ON SOLID GROUND

THE CHRISTIAN BASICS

Timothy K. Alspach

WinePress Publishing
MUKILTEO, WA 98275

To Susan, my best friend.

—— *Acknowledgments* ——

Here is a big thank you to some of the dear people who made this project fun and exciting, as well as possible.

To Tom and Paula Hess: You have been my biggest fans and a great encouragement.

To Bobby and Rebecca Whitlock: Your hospitality, patience, and computer skills helped me greatly.

To John Hamilton, Vern Salter, Bill Mason, Phil Partin, Dave Coffield, Mike Darnell: Thank you for taking time out of your busy schedules to read and offer suggestions as this project unfolded.

To Dana Murray. Thank you for using the book in your Bible study and for writing the study questions. Your help was much appreciated.

To the chaplains of the 82nd Airborne Division. Thank you for your support and desire to serve God. All the way!

Contents

Foreword

But they that wait upon the Lord shall renew their strength. They shall mount up with wings like eagles; they shall run and not be weary; they shall walk and not faint. (Isaiah 40:31)

On July 8, 1997, eight paratroopers from the 82nd Airborne Division lost their lives when a UH-60 Black Hawk helicopter crashed at Fort Bragg, North Carolina. The 2nd Battalion, 82nd Aviation Brigade helicopter crew; three paratroopers from the 313th Military Intelligence Battalion; and a flight surgeon from the 1-17 Cavalry were conducting an aerial photo mission when the helicopter went down. These soldiers gave their lives in the service of the United States of America. Their service to our country and to us shall always be remembered. That was the day that Captain Timothy K. Alspach, author of this book, answered the final call to our Lord.

Even on the day that Tim ended his earthly life, the blessings from God continued to abound. As our family arrived at Tim's home at Fort Bragg, we felt nothing but the love of God and the peace that He provided. Time after time, we were told of the impact Tim had made on the lives of so many—everyone from young eighteen-year-old PFCs to generals, commanders and staff personnel, the chaplain community and Navigators staff.

The one praise we heard over and over was about the service that this humble man offered his fellow man, not only by way of the field of medicine, but more importantly through his love of Christ. He had a consistent hunger to learn more and more of the Word of God, and he was always willing to share his own knowledge with whomever wanted to listen and learn. His wife said he considered this book to be a gift from the Lord and it is meant to lead others to an abundant Christian life.

My sister and I could continue to write endlessly about our brother, but what is important is that you know the kind of life he lived; and that is what this book is about.

Our brother loved to serve and he loved to love. He truly loved his Lord, his family and his country. He was a wonderful husband, father and brother in Christ. One memory that we will always cherish is that every conversation we had with Tim, on the phone or face to face, started and ended with "I love you!" So to our very special brother, "We love you!"

BILL ALSPACH
ALICE (ALSPACH) NEWLAND

——— *Preface* ———

It has been said that Vince Lombardi, one of the greatest NFL coaches and motivators of people, began each year's training camp by standing in front of his players, holding up a football, and saying, "Gentlemen, this is a football." Why did he get dramatic over something so rudimentary, so obvious? Because he believed that if his team knew the basics, practiced the basics, and performed the basics better than the other teams, they would win. His theory worked. In 1968 the Green Bay Packers won the NFL Championship. They are a testimony to the importance of the basics.

In the same manner, I strongly believe in the basics of the Christian life. Victorious Christian living comes from knowing, practicing, and performing the basics of Christianity.

You are probably asking yourself, "Why another book on Christian basics?" I asked myself the same question. The answer is threefold: First of all, in my prayer life, God is stressing these areas to me and urging me to write about them. I have no choice but to be obedient.

Second, I remember sitting in Xenos Fellowship several years ago listening to Gary Delashmut preach on the importance of the Word of God. He said that as he was preparing his teaching, the thought came to him that most of the people in the audience would already be Christians and know how important God's Word is. He almost decided to teach on a different subject. When I heard that sermon, I had been a Christian for twelve years, yet I had not seriously studied, meditated on, or memorized Scripture. Because Gary was faithful to God's leading and preached on God's Word, my life has been changed by the Bible.

Third, our Western Christian culture has gotten away from the basics and become more of a social gathering that emphasizes image, as opposed to the group of hardened spiritual warriors full of character that we're meant to be. It is my hope that, if you are a non-Christian, this book will challenge you to investigate this life we call "Christianity" and to accept Christ. If you are a Christian, I hope it will challenge you to return to the basics and help you to grow into a deeper relationship with Jesus.

Having spent several years in the military, I know there are tasks a commander considers essential for his soldiers to know if his unit is to be successful. If the unit is a medical unit, the soldiers need to be able to practice and do emergency treatment and evacuation of casualties. An infantry unit commander, on the other hand, wants his soldiers to be able to maneuver, take terrain, and engage and destroy the enemy in a proficient manner. In the same way, I chose the topics that are mission-essential tasks for the Christian life, ones I have found important in my life and in the lives of other Christians I love and respect.

Some call these basic principles "the means of grace"; others call them "the fundamentals of faith." Whatever we call them, if we want to be successful—success meaning being in step with and carrying out God's purposes—in the Christian life, we must as a unit, or body, get back to the following:

1. A personal relationship with Jesus
2. Prayer
3. Precepts of God
4. People
5. Purity and obedience
6. Perseverance
7. Praise and worship
8. Power from the Holy Spirit

These basics are not put forth as a quick fix or an easy way out. While they may seem simplistic, I assure you that carrying them out daily requires sacrifice.

As a physician's assistant, I see patients and prescribe medicines or treatments for them. Most people want a drug or therapy that will make them well *now*. But the body does not work that way, and neither does the Christian life. Just as two weeks of basic training do not make you a soldier, so two weeks of focusing on the above do not make you a mature Christian.

In the Army, the tasks required of soldiers are broken down into what are called skill levels. Skill-level one is for beginners, skill-level two is for intermediate soldiers, and skill-level three is for advanced soldiers. At first glance, this breakdown looks appropriate, but many people tend to assume that someone who can do level three skills can also do level-one skills. While this is normally the case, occasionally a soldier progresses up through the ranks and becomes proficient with the upper level administrative skills and rusty on the day-to-day soldiering skills of level one.

Christians can do the same thing. As we grow spiritually mature, we tend to shift our focus from the basics and concentrate on counseling, teaching, administering, pastoring, or whatever God has given us to do. It is my prayer that as you read this book you'll be called not to the new things but to become firmly established in the basics. And may the result be a life-changing meeting with Christ.

CHAPTER 1

A Personal Relationship
with Jesus

I remember it as if it happened yesterday. My mom and dad faithfully took me and my brother and sister to the Hopewell United Methodist Church every Sunday, and July 9, 1972, was no different. I entered the church that day as a fourteen-year-old boy confused about life, angry at the world, and frustrated that the harder I tried to be good, the more trouble I got into.

Rev. Harry Hill did an unselfish thing that Sunday morning. Instead of preaching himself, he turned the pulpit over to a sixteen-year-old young lady named Jan Vermeer, who had just come back from EXPLO '72, a rally sponsored by Campus Crusade for Christ. She had accepted Christ at the rally, and that morning in church she told me that God loved me, that I was a sinner and separated from Him and His love, and that if I would pray and ask Jesus to come into my heart, Jesus and His love would come in and never leave.

She was right. I asked Jesus to come into my heart that morning. There were no lights, no tears, no angels, no voices. Jesus simply came in, the confusion cleared, the anger melted, and the frustration left. Though my life, as well as my Christian walk, has had its ups and downs, good days and bad, He has always been faithful to me and has never left me. He is a rock, a solid stable foundation for anyone who desires Him.

As you read my testimony above, you may have wondered how I knew Jesus came into my heart. There were three things that happened immediately that assured me then and assure me now of Christ's residence in my heart: (1) I had a new interest in and desire for God's Word; (2) the inner turmoil was gone; and (3) by far the most significant, the "personable-ness" of Jesus. God was no longer an entity out in space some-where, or Someone I thought about only on Sundays, or a God who noticed me only when I messed up. He became personal and real to me.

In a day and age when computers enable us to shop, bank, and communicate without personal interaction, and when answering machines, voice mail, and automated service lines cause us to be surprised when a real person actually answers the phone, it is hard to think of God—Whom we cannot see with our eyes, hear with our ears, or touch with our hands—as a personal God. Yet He is! God is a personal God. I say it again, *God is a personal God.*

In Genesis 1:27–28 we read:

> So God created man in his own image, in the image of God he created him; male and female he created them. God blessed them and said to them, "Be fruitful and increase in number; fill the earth and subdue it...."

First, we see that we bear the image of God and, while it is true that some of us are more comfortable with personal rela-tionships than others, we as human beings are personal in nature. It stands to reason, then, that if we are personal and are created in God's image, one of His characteristics is that of personal-ness.

Second, God created us male and female, designed for interpersonal relationships. Again it seems logical that if God made us for interpersonal relating, He too has the capability of being personal.

David knew this too. Let's take a look at Psalm 18:2:

> The Lord is my rock, my fortress, and my deliverer; my God is my rock, in whom I take refuge. He is my shield and the horn of my salvation, my stronghold.

Notice the use of the personal pronoun *my*. The God called YAHWEH was personal to David. To David God was not *a* God or *the* God, but *my* God. Can you say that? That Jesus is your God?

David shows again the personal nature of God in verse 6 of the same Psalm:

> In my distress I called to the Lord; I cried to my God for help. From his temple he heard my voice; my cry came before him, into his ears.

Let's look at the two aspects of this verse that show God's personal-ness. First, God was the One David ran to when he was in trouble and at the end of his rope. I don't know about you, but when I am in trouble or in need of counsel or advice, I go to God first and then to the person(s) who is understanding, caring, and personable. We go to God in our crises because He is the author of personhood, and we know that His perfection in personhood is what we need to help us through those crises.

Second, observe that *God heard David!* From among the noises of David's days, the yelling and bartering of the marketplace, the cries of anguish from the tribal conflicts, and the joyous celebrations of the festivals and feasts, God heard the solitary voice of David. One of the most personal expressions we can show someone is listening—and God listens to us.

The last few verses we will look at in Psalm 18 are verses 16 and 17:

> He reached down from on high and took hold of me; he drew me out of deep waters. He rescued me from my powerful enemy, from my foes, who were too strong for me.

Notice the words used in these verses: *reached down, took hold of me, drew me, rescued me.* All of them reveal the personal interaction between God and David. God does these things for you too. He reaches down to take hold of you and draw you to His heart and rescue you from whatever situation you are in.

When I think of reaching down, I immediately think of my children, Joseph, Holly, and Brendan. When I get home from work, they run to the door and clamor for my attention with their arms outstretched, crying, "Hold me, hold me!" One at a time, I reach down and pick them up and give them hugs and kisses. I also do that when they've fallen down and skinned their knees or elbows. It is a fun, joyous, loving act on my part.

When God reaches down to us, it is different in only one aspect. His love and joy are perfected. God not only reaches down to pick us up, but He also takes hold of us. During my junior high wrestling days I wrestled heavyweight in an event in which I was matched against a young man who weighed more than I did, was stronger and faster than I was, and had more experience and moves than I did. Needless to say, I did not do too well that day. Once he took hold of me in that match, no matter what I did, I could not get away or gain the upper hand.

When God gets a hold on us, He is no different, and we cannot get away. He will not let us go, no matter what. That is comforting to know in today's world, when countries fall at a single shot, when people are unfaithful to us in word or deed. When circumstances around us are chaotic, it is grand to know that the God of the universe has a hold on us and will not let go.

Lest you think the personableness of God is limited only to the Old Testament, let's turn to Matthew 8:5–13:

> When Jesus had entered Capernaum, a centurion came to him, asking for help. "Lord," he said, "my servant lies at home paralyzed and in terrible suffering."
>
> Jesus said to him, "I will go and heal him." The centurion replied, "Lord, I do not deserve to have you come under my roof. But just say the word, and my servant will be healed. For I myself am a man under authority, with soldiers under me. I tell this one, 'Go,' and he goes; and that one, 'Come,' and he comes. I say to my servant, 'Do this,' and he does it."
>
> When Jesus heard this, he was astonished and said to those following him, "I tell you the truth, I have not found anyone in Israel with such great faith. I say to you that many will come from the east and the west, and will take their places at the feast with Abraham, Isaac, and Jacob in the kingdom of heaven. But the subjects of the kingdom will be thrown outside, into the darkness, where there will be weeping and gnashing of teeth."
>
> Then Jesus said to the centurion, "Go! It will be done just as you believed it would." And his servant was healed at that very hour.

The centurion came to Jesus asking for help. This centurion was not one of God's chosen people. He was not a religious leader or one of the disciples. He was one of the oppressors of the Jewish nation. Yet, in spite of all that, he felt comfortable approaching Jesus and asking for help.

It is probably because I am a soldier that I identify with this man so much. He was a centurion, a Roman soldier who had proved his skill as a soldier and leader and was placed in charge of one hundred men. Now, get this picture: Here is a man in charge of a hundred men who walks up to the God of the universe, the One who controls life and death, the One who controls sickness and health, the One who is in authority over all the angels and demons, and he asks for help. This tells me that one of two things took place. Either the centurion was a man of great courage, or Jesus was exceedingly accessible and approachable. I think it was probably a combination of the two, but the important fact here is that Jesus, God incarnate, was and is approachable. This approachability again shows God's personal side.

Next, Jesus commended the man in public for his faith. I have been given a public compliment only a couple of times in my life, and I can recall how grateful I was to the person who paid it. He made me feel esteemed, appreciated as a person, and important. Jesus did that for the Roman soldier. This shows that He understood the importance of affirmation and feeling valued as a person. Jesus Christ showed His personal side again.

Lastly, in this scene Jesus did what the man desired: He listened to him. He did not stop the man and say, "Listen, I'm the spiritual authority here and I say I'll come to your house and do it my way." Instead, He listened to the man and granted his request *as* he requested it. In my opinion, there isn't a more personable or more loving act than to listen genuinely to someone, and Jesus illustrated that in these verses.

God is personable. He will communicate with you. He has made you personal in nature, in His image, and He wants to be your personal God and relate to you in a personal way.

We are around people all the time. We have families—fathers, mothers, brothers, sisters, spouses, children, grandparents, aunts, uncles. We have friends—neighbors, classmates, army buddies, professional acquaintances. We have co-workers—supervisors, peers, subordinates. Yet, in the midst of the crowds, surrounded by people, one of the major problems today is loneliness, according to psychologists and psychiatrists. We're around people, but we do not relate to people. We do not have close interpersonal relationships.

Funk and Wagnalls Dictionary defines the word *relationship* as "the state of being related, connected, kinship suggestive of mutual regard and affection." Just as we do not relate well to each other, we also have a hard time relating to God. The question that is easily raised is: "If I have difficulty relating to people—individuals that I can see, hear, touch, and respond to—how do I relate to a God who is Spirit and whom I cannot see, hear, or touch in a physical sense?"

The answer to that question will be answered as you read the rest of this book, because prayer, Bible study, fellowship with God's people, praising God, and following the leading of the Holy Spirit are the answer to that question.

Another question that is raised is, "Does God want to relate to me, and if He does, will He meet my needs for a relationship?" The Bible is full of examples that shout yes to that question. Yes, God wants a relationship with you, and He wants to meet your relational needs.

The most poignant portrayal of this desire by God to have a relationship with us is found in Luke 8:42–48:

> …As Jesus was on his way, the crowds almost crushed him. And a woman was there who had been subject to bleeding for twelve years, but no one could heal her. She came up behind him and touched the edge of his cloak, and immediately her bleeding stopped.
>
> "Who touched me?" Jesus asked. When they all denied it, Peter said, "Master, the people are crowding and pressing against you." But Jesus said, "Someone touched me; I know that power has gone out from me."
>
> Then the woman, seeing that she could not go unnoticed, came trembling and fell at his feet. In the presence of all the people, she told why she had touched him and how she had been instantly healed. Then he said to her, "Daughter, your faith has healed you. Go in peace."

This episode in Jesus' life took place when He was on his way to heal a dying child. It was not as if He had nothing to do. There was a sense of urgency in the air as they made their way to heal Jairus's daughter. Yet, Jesus stopped the entire production. "Wait, someone touched Me," He said. In the midst of His busy life, He was unwilling to let one woman who touched Him in faith get by without a face-to-face, encouraging talk. He could've kept on walking. Both He and the woman already knew that she was healed. The woman apparently went unnoticed by the crowd, and she did not expect Jesus to stop. Yet, He did. Jesus desired a relationship with her that was more than a touch in the crowd. He wanted her to know that He cared for her. See how He calls her daughter—that was not by accident. Jesus placed her in a position where she was related to Him, a kinship in which she would recognize that she was regarded with high esteem and affection.

Jesus desires that kind of relationship with you and me today. That is why the Bible says that when we accept Jesus as Lord and Savior we become adopted sons of God. As children of God, Jesus places us in a position where we're related to Him, and He wanted this relationship so badly that He died for it.

The idea that God wanted me became crystal clear to me several years ago when I was praying and meditating on John 15:16.

> "You did not choose me, but I chose you and appointed you to go and bear fruit—fruit that will last."

God chose me, this verse says. For me, to be chosen is very special. When I was in elementary school, I had two physical problems. One was that I was overweight, and the other was that I had astigmatism, an eye disorder that kept me from judging distances well. These two problems, plus the fact that I was naturally uncoordinated, caused me considerable difficulty in playing football, basketball, baseball, or any other type of sport that required hand/eye coordination. As a result, during recess or PE whenever teams were chosen, I was usually picked last. I was not wanted, selected, or chosen. Yet, here God is saying that He has chosen me.

While I was meditating on John 15:16, I felt loved, needed, appreciated, affirmed, and connected to God all at the same time. Although I had been a Christian a long time, this experience made my Christianity very real to me. I now knew that God wanted a personal relationship with me, no strings attached.

The foundation of Christianity—the aspect of it that is unique and sets it apart from all other religions—is the idea that God, in the form of Jesus Christ, came to earth and died in our place that we might be made righteous and able have a personal relationship with God.

"Why do you call me, 'Lord, Lord,' and do not do what I say? I will show you what he is like who comes to me and hears my words and puts them into practice.

He is like a man building a house, who dug down deep and laid the foundation on rock. When a flood came, the torrent struck that house but could not shake it, because it was well built. But the one who hears my words and does not put them into practice is like a man who built a house on the ground without a foundation. The moment the torrent struck that house, it collapsed and its destruction was complete." (Luke 6:46–49)

"Why do you call me, 'Lord, Lord?'" What an intriguing question. The very fact that Christ asked it shows that His audience did not know Him as the Lord of their lives. They were obeying someone or something else. The central question that Christ asked here, that He illustrated with the parable, that is paramount in your life and mine, and that must be asked as we look at the Christian basics, is, "Who or what do I build my life upon?"

What's the foundation of your life? What's the basis of your life and existence? Our society does not like to ask those types of questions. Commercials say to us, "Why ask why?" or "Just do it!" inferring that the actions of life are more important than what we base our lives upon. This idea could not be further from the truth. The reason our society is so morally adrift is that we never take the time to ask why we're doing what we're doing.

All of us have a lord of some type. That lord determines how we live. If our lord is money, we will do whatever we can to put more green in our pockets. If our lord is power or fame, we will try to make all the right connections and attend all the proper social events so we can be seen with influential people. If our lord is religion, we will spend our time going to church and trying to do good. If our Lord is Jesus, we will serve and obey Him in a personal relationship no matter the cost.

As Luke portrayed in the parable of Jesus, if you are building a house, the most important issue and the first thing that must be settled is the foundation. So, too, if we plan to live the Christian life, the most important issue we must settle is, "Who is our Lord? Do we have a personal relationship with Jesus?"

You may read this and ask yourself, "Is this really that important?" Believe me, it is. Maybe you are a senator or mayor or other elected official and you make decisions that affect the way your state, city, or department is run. Maybe you are a nurse or a doctor and you make life-and-death decisions. Maybe you are a professor or teacher whose decisions today influence the leaders of tomorrow. Maybe you are a young person planning to get married soon and you must live with that person the rest of your life. You think, "How can anything be more important than these decisions?"

The decision you make when you face Jesus and either deny Him or choose to have a personal relationship with Him is so important that the other decisions pale in comparison. This is true for two reasons: First, what you decide about Jesus has eternal consequences for your soul—you'll go to either Heaven or Hell. Secondly, all of your subsequent decisions will in some way be influenced by this decision. If you are a senator and Christ is your Lord, how you vote on the laws about pornography and parents' rights will be different than if power and influence were your lord. If you are a doctor or nurse whose Lord is Jesus, taking part in an abortion or in the harvesting of fetal tissue will be unthinkable, as opposed to the doctor whose lord is money and who finances his car with the proceeds of an abortion clinic. I think you get the idea.

The three points I hope you've gotten so far are:

1. God is a personal God.
2. God desires a relationship with you through Jesus Christ.
3. A relationship with Jesus is the foundation of Christianity.

If you do not know Jesus personally, I urge you to accept Him into your heart today and begin this relationship. If you need help or do not understand how to accept Jesus, just read through the following section or contact the Navigators at (719) 598-1212.

How to Accept Jesus as Your Savior

1. Realize that all of us, including you, are sinners. Read Romans 3:23.
2. Understand that the penalty, or the wages of our sin, is death. Read Romans 6:23.
3. Know that no matter how many good or righteous things you do, they are not good enough to get you to Heaven. Read Titus 3:5.
4. Realize that Jesus died on the cross for your sins. Read I Peter 3:18 and Romans 5:8.
5. Believe that Jesus will save you, and invite Him into your heart. Read John 3:16–18 and Revelation 3:20.
6. Pray the following prayer, or something similar:

"Dear Jesus, I realize that I have been living my life on my own, by my rules, and without You. I know that this has been wrong and I ask for Your forgiveness. Thank You for dying on the cross for me so that I could have a relationship with You.

Please come into my life and help me to grow closer to You in this new relationship. Amen."

Questions for Chapter 1

1. Read II Corinthians 1:21–22. According to these verses, what action does God take in a believer's life?

2. Is it possible for a believer to lose his salvation?

3. Read John 14:23–24. How does Jesus know that we love him? What does Jesus promise in verse 23?

----------- CHAPTER 2 -----------

Prayer: Part One

In a marriage relationship, if the lines of communication are not kept open, eventually the relationship will flounder and most likely fail. If a person does not invest letters, cards, phone calls, and occasional visits in a friend who lives in a distant city, the feelings of closeness will eventually fade and contact with that friend will be lost. If a soldier on the battlefield gets isolated behind enemy lines with no means of communication with headquarters, he has become ineffective and is in a perilous position.

Likewise, in the Christian life, if we do not communicate with God, our relationship with Christ will suffer, our feelings of acceptance by God will fade, and our walk with Christ will become ineffective. In that light, we as Christians need to understand the important role of prayer (communicating with God) in our daily lives.

First of all, Scripture is quite clear on this matter. It commands us to pray. I Thessalonians 5:17 says:

> Pray continually, give thanks in all circumstances, for this is God's will for you in Christ Jesus.

And Colossians 4:2 commands us:

> Devote yourselves to prayer, being watchful and thankful.

God must consider prayer vitally important to us or He would not have commanded us to be devoted to it continuously.

Secondly, praying is one of God's ways of bestowing blessings upon us. We can see this in Luke 11:1–4, 9–13:

> One day Jesus was praying in a certain place. When he finished, one of his disciples said to him, "Lord, teach us to pray, just as John taught his disciples." He said to them, "When you pray, say: 'Father, hallowed be your name, your kingdom come. Give us each day our daily bread. Forgive us our sins, for we also forgive everyone who sins against us. And lead us not into temptation.'
>
> "…So I say to you: Ask and it will be given to you; seek and you shall find; knock and the door will be opened to you. For everyone who asks receives; he who seeks finds; and to him who knocks, the door will be opened.
>
> "Which of you fathers, if your son asks for a fish, will give him a snake instead? Or if he asks for an egg, will give him a scorpion? If you then, though you are evil, know how to give good gifts to your children, how much more will your Father in heaven give the Holy Spirit to those who ask him!"

God desires to bless us. It is my opinion that among other things, this Scripture is God's way of saying, "Talk to Me, share with Me your hopes and dreams, let Me be your Daddy, let Me be intimate with you and you be intimate with Me." Does this passage mean that if we do not ask or seek or knock God will not bless us? Definitely not! God has already given us the free gift of salvation through His Son, Jesus Christ; He has given His Holy Word in the Bible so we can come to know Him;

family and friends to share our lives with; and life itself. All we must do is accept it. God is telling us through this passage the invaluable importance of prayer.

Thirdly, prayer is vital to our balanced spiritual growth. Spiritual maturity comes as God develops us through Bible study, fellowship, ministry and outreach, and the rest of the basics we are going to talk about. These areas are all equally important to our growth, but, more than that, they are interrelated. Imagine trying to study the Bible without asking for God's understanding and perspective, or reaching out to someone without praying for God's divine insight into that person's life. So, God again emphasizes the importance of prayer by coupling it with spiritual growth.

Fourth, the old statement, "When Christians pray, the devil trembles," shows how valuable prayer is as a weapon in our spiritual battle. Philippians 4:6–7 says,

> Do not be anxious about anything, but in everything, by prayer and petition, with thanksgiving, present your requests to God. And the peace of God, which transcends all understanding, will guard your hearts and your minds in Christ Jesus.

God's peace guards us against Satan's accusations and the temptations of this world. Prayer is again stressed by Paul as a weapon when he concludes his instructions on spiritual armor this way:

> And pray in the spirit on all occasions with all kinds of prayers and requests. With this in mind, be alert and always keep on praying for all the saints (Ephesians 6:18).

Again, by placing prayer in our spiritual arsenal, we see the importance God places on prayer.

The last and most powerful argument for Christians to be in prayer is the priority that the apostles and Jesus gave to their prayer lives. In the sixth chapter of the book of Acts, the church was growing rapidly and the physical needs of all the members were not being met. The apostles thought it best that they give their attention to prayer and teaching the Word and turn the responsibility of meeting the physical needs over to seven men who were full of the Holy Spirit and wisdom. The result of their strategy was the fulfilling of the needs, the pleasing of the group of believers, and the continued rapid spreading of the gospel in Jerusalem. The apostles considered prayer so important that they ranked it among the highest priorities in their lives.

In Luke 5:15 we see that Jesus made prayer a high priority:

> Yet the news about him spread all the more, so that crowds of people came to hear him and to be healed of their sicknesses. But Jesus often withdrew to lonely places and prayed.

Christ was willing to let crowds of people who had needs and hurts and questions wait so that He could be alone and pray. He did this not because He was inconsiderate or lacked compassion, but because He gave prayer a high priority in His life. If we are to be effective for Christ, we too must recognize the importance of prayer and afford it a proper place in our priorities.

Having been shown the importance of prayer in the previous paragraph, we are now faced with the following question: "How do we approach God in this process of prayer, and upon what basis can we come to God in prayer?" Scripture screams on every page that we can approach God through faith in the grace of Jesus Christ. Hebrews 4:14–16 states:

> Therefore, since we have a great high priest who has gone through the heavens, Jesus the Son of God, let us hold firmly to the faith we profess. For we do not have a high priest who is unable to sympathize with our weaknesses,

but we have one who has been tempted in every way, just as we are—yet was without sin. Let us then approach the throne of grace with confidence, so that we may receive mercy and find grace to help us in our time of need.

In the Jewish tradition, the high priest acted as a mediator between God and the Israelites. The high priest would annually take the sin of the people on himself, make a sacrifice for those sins, and enter the Holy of Holies behind the curtain in the temple to secure God's forgiveness for the people. Jesus, the fulfillment of this Old Testament tradition Who took on the role of both the high priest and the sacrifice, has enabled us to approach God's throne with confidence based upon His work and grace. We see this idea expressed again in Hebrews 10:19–23:

> Therefore, brothers, since we have confidence to enter the most Holy Place by the blood of Jesus, by a new and living way opened for us through the curtain, that is, his body, and since we have a great priest over the house of God, let us draw near to God with a sincere heart in full assurance of faith, having our hearts sprinkled to cleanse us from a guilty conscience and having our bodies washed with pure water. Let us hold unswervingly to the hope we profess, for he who promised is faithful.

According to the writer of Hebrews, the answer to our question of how and upon what basis we approach God is this: We can come to God with assurance and confidence through faith in the grace of Christ.

As we come to God with confidence based upon His grace, we also need to come with purpose. If a sea-going vessel has no port of call, no destination, there is no purpose in its voyage. If we have no goal or ambition in life, we are said to have no direction or purpose in life. A ship without a destination, a life with no ambition, and a prayer without purpose are all ineffective and inefficient. With this in mind, let us look at Paul and Peter, two of the most effective Christian workers in the Bible, and see if we can detect their purpose in prayer.

> Now to him who is able to do immeasurably more than all we ask or imagine, according to his power that is at work within us, to him be glory in the church and in Christ Jesus throughout all generations, for ever and ever! Amen. (Ephesians 3:20–21)

> And this is my prayer: that your love may abound more and more in knowledge and depth of insight, so that you may be able to discern what is best and may be pure and blameless until the day of Christ, filled with the fruit of righteousness that comes through Jesus Christ—to the glory and praise of God. (Philippians 1:9–11)

> But grow in the grace and knowledge of our Lord and Savior Jesus Christ. To him be glory both now and forever! Amen. (II Peter 3:18)

Paul and Peter's purpose in prayer was to bring glory to God. As we become imitators of Paul and Peter and develop this purpose into an attitude of prayer, our prayer lives become more effective and focused on God. If our goal is to bring glory to Christ, we will be kept from praying with wrong motives, as we are warned in James 4:3–6, and will experience a more joyful prayer life. As we learn to pray with the purpose of glorifying God, our prayers will change from requests for what will bring us pleasant feelings, comfort, and easy living to prayers that will do the most for God's purpose (saving and sanctifying men) and will bring Him the most glory by further demonstrating His grace.

By relating to Christ and embarking on these adventures of prayers with Him, we will begin to see that prayer changes things. Sometimes God intervenes and changes circumstances, and sometimes, instead of changing circumstances, He changes the person or people in the situations. Still other times He works by changing both. In Luke 9 we see Jesus feeding five thousand men with two fish and five loaves of bread. He changed circumstances to meet the peoples' needs and fulfill His purposes. In Mark 9 Jesus drove out evil forces and released a boy from a demon. In John 11, where Jesus raised Lazarus from the dead, we see God changing circumstances in answer to prayer.

These are all examples of God performing miracles in answer to prayer for His glory. If you are like me, you are saying to yourself that Christ was God and man, so when He prayed, naturally, things would happen. Christ is not the only one who prayed and found circumstances altered. Abraham, who gave his wife to a king so he would not be killed, prayed, and God spared Lot from Sodom and Gomorrah. He prayed again and received a son in his old age. Moses, who murdered an Egyptian with his own hands, prayed and brought the Egyptians under various plagues. He prayed again and the Red Sea was parted. James 5:17–18 puts it this way:

> Elijah was a man just like us. He prayed earnestly that it would not rain, and it did not rain on the land for three and a half years. Again he prayed, and the heavens gave rain, and the earth produced its crops.

The patriarchs of old were no different from us, and God is just as able to intervene today in our situations in supernatural ways if it suits His purposes. Prayer changes circumstances.

God is also interested in developing our character and changing our attitudes. Many times, instead of changing circumstances, He allows the circumstances to change us and thereby answers our prayer—just not in the way we were expecting Him to. Following is a list of ways that prayer can affect the one who is praying. It is not meant to be an exhaustive list.

1. Change fear and anguish to hope and boldness. (Read Psalm 2.18:5–7.)
3. Develop strength and boldness. (Read Psalm 138:3.)
4. Change one from a lost state to a state of deliverance. (Read Joel 2:32.)
5. Develop joy. (Read John 16:24.)
6. Change feelings of anxiety to peace of mind and heart. (Read Philippians 4:4–6.)
7. Develop wisdom. (Read James 1:5.)

In studying the prayers of the Bible, one is struck with two distinct types of prayers. The first type I call casual prayer. This kind of prayer relates to specific situations, takes place in response to current events, and is usually short and concise. The second type I call intimate prayer and is more protracted and "worked at"; the Bible calls it a wrestling-type prayer. (Read about Jacob in Genesis 32:22, and Epaphras in Colossians 4:12.) This type of prayer takes time, is often more long-term, and is focused on spiritual warfare rather than physical events and circumstances. An illustration of these two types of prayer is the intimate human relationship and the communication process. Both casual and intimate levels of communication exist in close relationships. Both are necessary, and neither one is more important than the other.

For example, in a marriage, casual conversation takes place every day. "How was your day?" "Fine, how was work?" and so on. This kind of communication, which takes place at random times throughout the day, is spontaneous and deals with issues directly at hand. It is normal and keeps the lines of communication open. Without this type of communication, the little issues of everyday life build up until they are major issues, possibly leading to a total communication breakdown and fractured relationship.

A marriage relationship also needs periods of intimate communication if it is to be healthy. The same husband and wife that had the casual conversation may have to confront one another about a spiritual problem, encourage one another in ministry efforts, discuss the use of time and money in relation to their priorities, or confess sin to one another. These are all areas that require prayer, time, effort, and thought. In order for a marriage to be deep and close, time needs to be set aside for periods of intimate communication.

In our relationship with Christ, we too need both casual and intimate communication. In our daily walk with Him, we should converse with Him casually. We should thank him for our lives, our friends, the beauty of the day; call out to Him in emergencies and when we are tempted; talk to Him about situations at work, about acquaintances and their souls, or about a sick friend. Jesus did all of these in His relationship with His Father. He gave thanks before He fed the five thousand, He praised God for revealing Himself to the disciples (see Luke 10:21), and He prayed for the wind and sea to be calm.

This is not the only way Christ prayed, however. Take a look at Luke 22:39–43:

> Jesus went out as usual to the Mount of Olives, and his disciples followed him. On reaching the place, he said to them, "Pray that you will not fall into temptation." He withdrew about a stone's throw beyond them, and knelt down and prayed, "Father, if you are willing, take this cup from me; yet not my will, but yours be done." An angel from heaven appeared to him and strengthened him. And being in anguish, he prayed more earnestly, and his sweat was like drops of blood falling to the ground.

This is intimate prayer. We need times like this too.

Now that we know the importance of both casual and intimate prayer, we see that there are four themes, or characteristics, of prayer that apply to both: praise (adoration), seeking forgiveness, thankfulness, and making requests for both oneself and others.

The best way to describe adoration is to ask you to picture in your mind a mother and father holding their newborn baby for the first time. They are in awe of the new life given into their charge. They examine and fondle the child to begin to know it. They check out every finger and toe. They are overjoyed and full of love for this little one as the greatness of the miracle of life that has just come into the world crashes in upon them.

This is adoration. As we come to God in prayer, our undeservedness of the privilege and His great mercy should bring a sense of awe and wonderment. His righteousness is worthy of our praise. Now I am not advocating that we work ourselves up into an emotional frenzy, and neither am I suggesting that we suppress the emotions God has given us. I am simply saying that as we approach God we should see ourselves for who we are and God for who He is and what He has done for us through His Son. Prayer, after all, is spending time with God. As we grow in prayer and do this more often, His worthiness and our adoration of Him will increase. Reading the Psalms is helpful in developing this aspect of prayer. (See Psalms 8; 9:1–2; 19:1–4; 29; 48:1–3; 66:1–4; 92:1–8; 106; 108; 117; 135; 138:1–2; 145; 147:1; 148; 149:1; and 150).

Another thing exhibited in prayers of the Bible is forgiveness. This deals with both confession and repentance (telling God our sins, feeling and showing sorrow for having committed them, and having a change of heart), as well as seeking the strength to forgive those who have hurt us.

As mentioned before, the third characteristic of the prayers of the Bible is thanksgiving. In developing a grateful and thankful heart, we would do well to emulate Paul. Notice the theme that goes through all of the prayers below:

> First, I thank my God through Jesus Christ for all of you, because your faith is being repeated all over the world. (Romans 1:8)

> I always thank God for you because of his grace given you in Christ Jesus. (I Corinthians 1:4)

> I have not stopped giving thanks for you, remembering you in my prayers. (Ephesians 1:16)

I thank my God every time I remember you. In all my prayers for all of you, always pray with joy because of your partnership in the gospel from the first day until now. (Philippians 1:3–5)

Paul was definitely a man with a thankful heart and a challenging example for us to follow.

The last characteristic of prayer is that of supplication and intercession: making requests to God for ourselves and others. This is the easiest part of prayer for most of us, and we have little if any problem coming up with things to ask God for. While it is important to develop a healthy balance of praise, forgiveness, thanksgiving, and petition in our casual and intimate prayer, remember above all else that prayer is simply talking with and listening to God with a sincere heart.

Questions for Chapter 2

1. Read I Thessalonians 5:17 and Colossians 4:2. Both of these verses direct us to be constant in our prayer. What else do these verses instruct us to do?

2. Read Matthew 6:9–13. What does Jesus' teaching on prayer tell us about the elements of prayer?

3. Read Philippians 4:6–7. What does God promise in these verses?

4. What was Peter and Paul's purpose in their prayers to God? Does this mean that they got what they asked for? What about their circumstances?

--- CHAPTER 3 ---

Prayer: Part Two

In chapter two we looked at the importance of, basis of, purpose of, effects of, and types of prayer. This is good information, but unless we apply the principles to everyday experiences and the reality of life, they will keep prayer on a surreal level. What about unanswered prayer? Exactly how do I pray? How do I develop prayer in other Christians? What about prayer meetings and praying in public? All of these are practical issues that we need to look at.

The question I hear most regarding prayer and the question I ask myself most often is, "What about unanswered prayer?" We've all had times when we've prayed and it seemed as though God was not there; it seemed that our prayers bounced off the ceiling and smacked us in the face. We all have family members, friends, and situations that we have been praying about for a long time, and it appears as though God hasn't heard or isn't interested in those prayers. At times like this, when we are discouraged, we must go back to God's Word. Psalm 139:1–4 says,

O Lord, you have searched me and you know me. You know when I sit and when I rise; you perceive my thoughts from afar. You discern my going out and my lying down; you are familiar with all my ways. Before a word is on my tongue you know it completely, O Lord.

If God knows our thoughts and the words we are going to speak, shouldn't He also know our prayers? Indeed, He does hear our prayers. Jesus said that our Heavenly Father knows what we need before we even ask for it. (See Matthew 6:8.) God hears and knows our prayers. When we encounter a seemingly impossible situation or a barrier in our prayer life, when it appears that God is not answering, we need to try to develop God's perspective on the issue.

For example, I learned about perspective in the Army when I became a paratrooper. When I jumped out of an airplane with a parachute on my back and looked at the ground below, rivers appeared to be silvery yarn stretched out beneath me, mountains looked like small hills, distances of miles seemed to be only inches, and buildings and cars looked like small dots. However, after I landed, those same rivers, mountains, miles, buildings, and cars went back to their normal size. It was a matter of perspective.

What appears to us as a mountain or river too huge or too deep to overcome, God sees as possible. When we are impatient and we think God is taking too long to answer us, look at the situation from the perspective of eternity. As we learn to pray, we need to develop an ability to see the answers to our prayers from God's perspective. As Proverbs 3:5–6 says,

Trust in the Lord with all your heart and lean not on your own understanding; in all your ways acknowledge him, and he will make your paths straight.

As with any kind of request, there are three possible answers to our requests made in prayer: yes, no, and wait. When we pray about an issue and God answers us quickly and with a yes, our faith is affirmed and our hopes soar. Most of us have little difficulty dealing with answers to prayer like this. But what about the prayer that is answered with a no? How do we deal with this? Do you do as I tend to do and see God as a killjoy, act like a spoiled child, and either pout, throw a temper tantrum, or run away? Or perhaps you barter with God: If I read my Bible more, or go to more Christian meetings, or witness more, maybe He'll change His mind. We need to realize that we cannot manipulate God. He is a concerned heavenly parent Who wants the best for us.

I have the privilege and challenge of being a parent, and I know that if my son were to ask me if he could use the car when he turns twelve, I would tell him no. Why? Because even if he were physically able to drive, the law says he must be sixteen; it would not be in his best interests to give him the keys.

On the same principle, God often tells us no because what we request is not in our best interests. We also need to look again at the purpose of prayer. The purpose of prayer is to bring glory to Jesus Christ, and since God has initiated prayer so that we can give glory to His Son, He will not answer our prayers if the answer will bring dishonor to His Son.

The last and probably most difficult answer to deal with is "wait." It is the most difficult answer because it is not definite; it leaves us with the question, "How long do I wait?" God does this not to be cruel or to dangle something in front of us, but to build our dependence on and faith in Him. He is strengthening and building our character.

Figure-skating competitions in the winter Olympics are always beautiful to watch. But the figure skaters did not become champions overnight. When they first began training, their coaches had them do simple things. First they learned how to do a simple cross-over move, then a simple jump. As they gained faith in their ability and as their muscles got stronger and developed more endurance, the coach introduced more difficult moves. After years of practice, they demonstrated the skill that enabled them to compete in the Olympics.

Just as the coach develops the skills of the skaters by testing and stretching their ability with more difficult jumps little by little, so God develops our faith by asking us to wait and depend on Him. David declares this in the Psalms:

> Wait for the Lord; be strong and take heart and wait for the Lord. (Psalm 27:14)

> I wait for the Lord, my soul waits, and in his word I put my hope. My soul waits for the Lord more than watchmen wait for the morning, more than watchmen wait for the morning. (Psalm 130:5–6)

The answer may be yes, no, or wait, but whatever it is, we can be certain God hears and answers every prayer.

As we look at the ministry of Jesus and the relationship He had with His disciples, we see that the only "how to" question recorded in Scripture is one that tells us how to pray. While I am sure the disciples asked many questions of Christ, it is interesting to note that God, as He inspired Scripture, ensured that Christ's response to the question, "Lord, teach us to pray," was included. Not, How do I teach, or, How do I lead, but, How do I pray, is what we have in Scripture. Keeping this thought in mind, let us look at some guidelines Scripture gives.

1. Deal with sin.

> Surely the arm of the Lord is not too short to save, nor his ears too dull to hear. But your iniquities have separated you from your God; your sins have hidden his face from you, so that he will not hear. For your hands are stained with blood, your fingers with guilt. Your lips have spoken lies, and your tongue mutters wicked things. (Isaiah 59:1–3)

In other words, it is not that God isn't big enough to answer our prayers, and it is not that He cannot hear our prayers, but it is that He is more interested in our hearts and changing us and having us confess our sins than in granting our requests. In this same light, look at what David said about sin in the Psalms:

Blessed is he whose transgressions are forgiven, whose sins are covered. Blessed is the man whose sin the Lord does not count against him and in whose spirit is no deceit. When I kept silent my bones wasted away through my groaning all day long. For day and night your hand was upon me; my strength was sapped as in the heat of summer. Then I acknowledged my sin to you and did not cover up my iniquity. I said, "I will confess my transgressions to the Lord"—and you forgave the guilt of my sin. (Psalm 32:1–5)

Have mercy on me, O God, according to your unfailing love; according to your great compassion blot out my transgressions. Wash away all my iniquity and cleanse me from my sin. For I know my transgressions, and my sin is always before me.

Against you, you only, have I sinned and done what is evil in your sight, so that you are proved right when you speak and justified when you judge. Surely I was sinful at birth, sinful from the time my mother conceived me. Surely you desire truth in the inner parts; you teach me wisdom in the inmost place.

Cleanse me with hyssop, and I will be clean; wash me, and I will be whiter than snow. Let me hear joy and gladness; let the bones you have crushed rejoice. Hide your face from my sins and blot out all my iniquity.

Create in me a pure heart, O God, and renew a steadfast spirit within me. Do not cast me from your presence or take your Holy Spirit from me. Restore to me the joy of your salvation and grant me a willing spirit to sustain me. (Psalm 51: 1–12)

2. Forgive others. Jesus told us to forgive others when we pray. Not only is our relationship with Him important, but so are our relationships with others. God's Word puts it this way:

> "And when you stand praying, if you hold anything against anyone, forgive him, so that your Father in Heaven may forgive you your sins." (Mark 11:25)

> "For if you forgive men when they sin against you your heavenly Father will also forgive you. But if you do not forgive men their sins, your father will not forgive your sins." (Matthew 6:14–15)

3. Pray with proper motives. James is pretty blunt in his letter to the church:

> You want something but do not get it. You kill and covet, but you cannot have what you want. You quarrel and fight. You do not have, because you do not ask God. When you ask, you do not receive, because you ask with wrong motives, that you may spend what you get on your pleasures. (James 4:2–3)

4. Have proper family relationships. In I Peter 3:7 Peter stressed that husbands are to be considerate of their wives and treat them with respect so that nothing will hinder their prayer lives.

5. Pray to God, not for the admiration of men. In Matthew 6:5–6 Jesus said,

> "And when you pray, do not be like the hypocrites, for they love to pray standing in the synagogues and on the street corners to be seen by men. I tell you the truth, they have received their reward in full. But when you pray, go into your room, close the door and pray to your Father, who is unseen. Then your Father, who sees what is done in secret, will reward you."

6. Persist in prayer. Jesus gave two poignant parables that deal with persistence. In Luke 11:5–8 we see a friend whose persistence and boldness caused his neighbor to get out of bed and meet the friend's needs. Along the same lines, in Luke 18:1–8 a widow who was being treated unfairly finally received justice from an unjust judge because of her persistence.

A question I always face when I look at these two parables is this: If God knows our prayers, thoughts, and needs even before we pray, and if He wants us to pray with faith, why would He want us to pray for something over and over again? I do not have a good answer; however, I do know that as I pray for people or situations over extended periods of time, several things happen. First, the longer I pray about a situation, the more grateful I am when my prayer is answered. Second, God uses the extended time as a screening process to give me more insight into situations and therefore bring my prayers more into alignment with His will. Third, God makes me become more dependent, and I grow closer to Him. Fourth, when God answers a prayer I have been praying for a long time, His faithfulness to me and the truth of His promises are reaffirmed. Finally, by my spending time with Jesus in prayer, my relationship with Him is made stronger.

7. Pray with humility. Continuing in Luke 18, Jesus says in verses 9–14,

> To some who were confident of their own righteousness and looked down on everybody else, Jesus told this parable, "Two men went up to the temple to pray, one a Pharisee and the other a tax collector. The Pharisee stood up and prayed about himself: 'God, I thank you that I am not like other men—robbers, evildoers, adulterers—or even like this tax collector. I fast twice a week and give a tenth of all I get.'
>
> "But the tax collector stood at a distance. He would not even look up to heaven, but beat his breast and said, 'God, have mercy on me, a sinner.'

"I tell you that this man, rather than the other, went home justified before God. For everyone who exalts himself will be humbled, and he who humbles himself will be exalted."

We need to be humble when we pray.

8. Pray with faith. Jesus said,

"...I tell you the truth, if you have faith and do not doubt, not only can you do what was done to the fig tree, but also you can say to this mountain, 'Go, throw yourself into the sea,' and it will be done. If you believe, you will receive whatever you ask for in prayer." (Matthew 21:21–22)

If we pray without faith, James tells us that we are as unstable as the waves of the sea. The writer of Hebrews says that without faith it is impossible to please God. If we are to pray with faith, we need to understand what it is. *The American College Dictionary* defines faith as a confidence or trust in a person or thing. The Bible defines it in Hebrews 11:1:

Now faith is being sure of what we hope for and certain of what we do not see.

As we look at these two definitions, we can see that faith is placing our trust in God and in His promises, regardless of what feelings, circumstances, or other people may say. It is believing that God is Who He says He is and then living our lives accordingly, trusting Christ to be our fulfillment.

There are also two things faith is not. First, faith is not a blind abandonment of all reason. Through history, archeology, and human experience God supports the claims of Scripture. Second, faith is not a form of positive thinking or a positive mental attitude. Positive thinking asserts that fulfillment comes when circumstances are perfect for me or just the way I want them. True and lasting fulfillment comes only from a right relationship with Jesus Christ, no matter what the circumstances. That is why Paul could rejoice when he was in prison. Positive thinking could not change the dungeon, but Paul's faith in God enabled him to endure and rejoice.

Now I would like to give some ideas that others have shared with me on developing a prayer life. These ideas are just helpful hints and are not meant to be observed as rigid rules. They are simply ideas that have helped me. In themselves these hints can do nothing, but if we submit them to God as we do them, He can use them in our lives. To get started, find a friend with whom you are comfortable and who has a faith in Jesus Christ. Agree to get together on a regular basis and pray about specific things in your lives. Be personal and intimate both with Jesus and one another.

Another helpful hint is to start a prayer list. Write down specific requests and, as answers come, write those down as well. As you go back and look at how God has answered prayers, your faith will be strengthened.

Something else that is similar to a prayer list is a prayer journal. This is a place where you can write down your feelings and express your emotions as best you can about your time with God. I have found this to be extremely helpful when I am going through a difficult time.

Still another hint is to set aside a specific time and place for prayer. Almost anything we want to accomplish requires a plan. If we want to get in shape, we set aside a time and place to exercise. If we want to build a friendship, we set aside a time and place so we can be with the person we are trying to befriend. If we want to commune with God in prayer, we need to set aside a time and place to do so.

Next, you can use Scripture in prayer. Find Scriptures passages that are important to you and pray them back to God in praise and worship. This not only helps us understand Scripture and, therefore, God, but it can also show us how to pray for specific situations as God speaks through His Word.

Lastly, try reading some books on prayer. These help us understand praying through the experience of others.

Another important and practical aspect of prayer is corporate prayer. Corporate prayer occurs when a group of believers comes together for the specific purpose of spending time in prayer. It is so important because it develops unity in the church by reaffirming, strengthening, informing, and ministering. As people pray together about common goals of ministry, they are drawn closer together. Since one of Satan's tactics is to divide and isolate believers so he can overcome them, praying with and for each other in corporate prayer creates important protection for the church body.

Paul considered this unity very important.

> If you have any encouragement from being united with Christ, if any comfort from his love, if any fellowship with the Spirit, if any tenderness and compassion, then make my joy complete by being like-minded, having the same love, being one in spirit and purpose. (Philippians 2:1–2)

What better way to develop this quality of unity than by praying together? Corporate prayer can and often does reaffirm what was just taught at the meeting. Often in my own experience, as someone is praying after a sermon and thanking God for an aspect of the teaching that touched his life, the Holy Spirit will drive home that same point to my heart as well.

We are also strengthened spiritually as we pray corporately. The author of Ecclesiastes declares in chapter 4, verses 9–12:

> Two are better than one, because they have a good return for their work: If one falls down, his friend can help him up. But pity the man who falls and has no one to help him up! Also, if two lie down together, they will keep warm. But how can one keep warm alone? Though one may be

overpowered, two can defend themselves. A cord of three stands is not quickly broken.

Corporate prayer not only strengthens us as a body of believers, but it also informs us. As individuals pray about their needs in a corporate prayer setting, the local church body is informed of mission needs, community needs, individual needs, and other situations that the church needs to pray over. As we are better informed about the needs of a brother or sister or mission field, we can pray (and act) in a more unified and specific way. As we minister to one another through actions and prayer, we grow stronger, and as we grow stronger we become more unified. It is all tied together. As we pray corporately, the unity, affirmation, strengthening, informing, and ministering that take place draw us together and form bonds of love that make us stand out to a world starved for that God-like type of love.

As we grow and develop in our Christian lives, we learn that if we try to hold onto a spiritual truth, it becomes stagnant and useless, but if we pass that truth on to others, it flourishes and becomes more effective. This is true of prayer also. As we learn more about prayer, we need to share with others and encourage them in their prayer life.

This leads us to an interesting question: "How do we motivate or encourage others to begin or develop a prayer life?" In order to answer this question, let us look at how Jesus answered it for His disciples. First, Christ was close to God the Father and to His disciples. He took the time and the effort to draw near to them both. Second, He prayed with them. He called Peter, James, and John to pray with Him at Gethsemane. Third, He prayed *for* them. John 17:6–19 gives an example of Christ praying for His disciples. Lastly, He led by example—He prayed. The disciples saw Him pray in the early morning, sometimes all night, before He fed the five thousand, and many other times. After a while they made the connection that part of Jesus' power for living as the Son of God came from His prayer life, so they asked Him to teach them how to pray. Notice that Jesus never ridiculed them for not praying, He never begged them to pray, He never manipulated them to pray—He simply prayed.

As we face this question of how to stir others to prayer, we can also look to Paul for some help. The thing that made Paul unique in this area of prayer was his vulnerability to his disciples and his requests for prayer. Listen to the requests of Paul:

> Brothers, pray for us. (I Thessalonians 5:25)

> Finally, brothers, pray for us that the message of the Lord may spread rapidly and be honored, just as it was with you. And pray that we may be delivered from evil and wicked men, for not everyone has faith. (II Thessalonians 3:1–2)

> Pray also for me, that whenever I open my mouth, words may be given so that I will fearlessly make known the mystery of the gospel, for which I am an ambassador in chains. Pray that I may declare it fearlessly, as I should. (Ephesians 6:19–20)

Paul was open and requested prayer humbly, shared his heart's vision for the lost, and told them of his hardship with his chains. We should also be so open and honest.

It is my hope that after reading these two chapters on prayer you will be encouraged to draw closer to Christ through prayer. Praying is not always easy; sometimes we do not know how or what to pray for, and at other times our emotions get in the way. Sometimes I just do not feel like it—I would rather watch TV. Because of that, many of us (myself included) neglect to draw near to God. In spite of the difficulty and hardship that sometimes is involved with prayer, the beauty and joy of meeting with Jesus in prayer makes the effort more than worthwhile.

It is important to remember this fact: If you do not pray, none of the material in these chapters will matter. You could memorize every verse in the Bible dealing with prayer, read every book in the Christian bookstore on prayer, and even teach workshops on prayer, but that is all vanity if you do not pray. As Samuel Chadwick says, "There is no way to learn to pray but by praying. No reasoned philosophy of prayer ever taught a soul to pray. The subject is beset with problems, but there are no problems of prayer to the man who prays."[1]

It is my earnest desire and sincere prayer that these two chapters on prayer will increase your excitement about knowing Christ and will cause you to spend more time with Him. May God bless you as you join with Him in this adventure called prayer.

Questions for Chapter 3

1. Read Proverbs 3:5–6. Why do you think we are told not to "lean" on our own understanding? What happens when we rely on common sense?

2. What happens when we pray to God without confessing our sins? Can you hide sin from God?

3. Read Matthew 6:14–15. Are we ever justified when we choose not to forgive someone? How does that affect our relationship with God?

4. Read Luke 18:9–14. What can happen when we compare ourselves to others? Why is a self-righteous attitude wrong?

5. Why is it essential for us to have faith when we pray? Does exercising faith mean we can "claim" a verse of scripture to change our circumstances?

---

1. *The Path of Prayer.* Christian Literature Crusade, Fort Washington, PA, p. 14.

—— CHAPTER 4 ——

Precepts of God—His Word

Have you ever had the experience of talking with someone when you have something else on your mind? Or maybe at work while talking with your superior you realize that he, through flattery, is trying to get you to do something you do not want to do. Maybe you can remember chatting with a friend who is from a different culture and at the end of the conversation you realize that the two of you did not really communicate well because of your different backgrounds.

All three of these instances are examples of poor communication. In the first example, the communication process broke down because the actual speech was irrelevant to your thought process. Your thoughts were different from the words being spoken. In the second example, the problem with the dialogue was lack of reliability. The compliment paid to you by your supervisor was not valid (it lost its reliability) because he had ulterior motives and was trying to manipulate you. In the third example, the lack of common ground prevented good communication.

Let's take a look at the other end of the communication spectrum. Try to picture two people who love each other and are dating. They talk about one another's hopes and dreams, ideas are exchanged effectively because the communication is relevant to both people, reliable, and shares the commonality of the relationship. In short, they are relating and communicating effectively and building a deeper relationship in the process. Their goal is to experience the other person to the fullest extent possible.

When we look at the Bible—God's communication and revelation to us—the communication process can be good or bad, just as it is in our relationships with people. In communicating with God, we see that a major part of this process is God's self-disclosure to us. It stands to reason, then, that because the Bible is the primary source of God's disclosure to us, we should strive to learn as much about the Book as possible. This forces us to ask, Is the Bible relevant, Is it reliable, and, Is it a form of communication common to us today?

From a personal point of view, I can tell you that the Scriptures are reliable. During one of the most difficult times in my life, I was rejected by someone I cared about deeply; I lost my job, the ministry effort I was involved in ceased, and my finances fell apart. My emotions were a wreck and my mental outlook was unstable. Everything in my life that I cared about and relied upon was gone—except for God and His Word. When I looked to the Bible, it never failed to uplift, encourage, strengthen, and set my thoughts back on the right track. The passage that encouraged and uplifted me most during that time was Jeremiah 29:11–12.

> "For I know the plans I have for you," declares the Lord, "plans to prosper you and not to harm you, plans to give you hope and a future. Then you will call upon me and come and pray to me, and I will listen to you. You will seek me and find me when you seek me with all your heart."

I will never forget the day I read those verses. It was the lowest day of my life, and I felt as if everyone, including God, had abandoned me and did not care or understand what I was going through. Tony Rowe, a friend of mine, gave me a piece of paper with that passage written on it. I read it over and over that day. Realizing that God had a plan and future for me that were good slowly renewed my hope. That was how God began to heal my life. I am still affected by that verse every time I read it. As I think of this experience, I am reminded of God's faithfulness to me through the Scriptures.

Another verse that had a big impact on my life during this time was Isaiah 41:10:

> So do not fear, for I am with you; do not be dismayed, for I am your God. I will strengthen you and help you; I will uphold you with my righteous right hand.

For someone who was afraid of trying, confused over the past, and too emotionally weak to help anyone, this was the perfect verse. God spoke to me through that verse exactly when I needed to hear it. Knowing that God's right hand was holding me up enabled me to face my fears, my past, and my weaknesses. Again God's promises proved reliable in my life. While my friends and family members have stood beside me during rough times, it was God's Word that was available and never-failing.

During my undergraduate days at Ohio University several professors told me that the Bible is a book of antiquity and therefore does not apply to today's society. They said it was not relevant to the twentieth-century man. They did not have their facts straight.

> "It is impossible to rightly govern the world without God and the Bible."
>
> —*George Washington*

> "Without Christ you will not have the foundation to resist temptations. You are going to be arrogant and self-centered without Christ, you will not be able to resist all this.

It is too powerful. Find out what is really important. Find out that God is real and trust Him."

—*David Robinson (Center for San Antonio Spurs,* Victory Magazine, *Special Issue 1996, page 11)*

"I believe the Bible is the best gift God has ever given to men. All the good of the Savior of the world is communicated through this book."

—*Abraham Lincoln*

"There are a good many problems before the American people today, and before me as President, but I expect to find the solutions of these problems just in the proportion that I am faithful in the study of the Word of God."

—*Woodrow Wilson*

"I do not know what it is like for people in other professions, but for the scientific mind, the Bible is wonderful if you read it from start to finish. It fits together with an astonishing consistency, which was the opposite of my secular perception...."

—*Dr. Raymond Damadian, pioneer of the MRI* (Physician Magazine, *May/June 1996, page 7, published by Focus on the Family)*

"The transition to life after pro football began when I accepted Jesus Christ into my life three years before the end of my career. At that time I began to focus on Jesus and my family rather than on myself. When I retired, I did not miss pro football. My identity was with Christ. Priorities had changed."

—*Paul Coffman, Green Bay Packer Hall of Famer* (Victory Magazine, *Special Issue 1996, page 27)*

The reason I listed these quotes is to show that the Bible has had an effect on history throughout the ages. The Bible has affected the way people live and think. It has influenced decisions that have been made throughout the years, because it has given guidelines, principles, and morals to the people making decisions. Also, some of these quotes were spoken by people who live in our time and are our contemporaries. If the Bible speaks to them as they say it does, then this Book, in spite of its antiquity, has bridged the gap of two thousand years and remained relevant.

Family values, homosexuality, abortion, suicide, child discipline, parenting skills, how to handle suffering, how to pick a spouse, making marriage relationships last, overcoming depression, making friends, establishing family values—all of these major issues are addressed in the Bible. Let me say that again: The Bible deals with all of the social and moral issues of our day. It is the handbook of life! The reason people in our society today call it irrelevant is not because the Bible does not deal with contemporary issues. It is because they do not want to acknowledge that there are moral absolutes and that their choices could be called sinful.

I can think of many times that, while reading the Bible, I have come across a verse I had read numerous times before but that had not had much impact on me until that particular reading. Then, because of my particular life circumstances, the verse jumped off the page. It became relevant to me at that time. The most recent time this happened to me was a couple of days ago while reading Jeremiah 9:23–24:

> This is what the Lord says, "Let not the wise man boast of his wisdom or the strong man boast of his strength or the rich man boast of his riches, but let him who boasts boast about this: that he understands and knows me, that I am the Lord, who exercises kindness, justice, and righteousness on earth, for in these I delight," declares the Lord.

I had read this verse many times before, but as I read it that time, it occurred to me that the Lord delights in exercising kindness. He delights in being kind to me. The God of the universe, Who deserves our respect, delights—not just likes or enjoys—in being kind to us. What a wonderful way for a verse to be relevant! Learning this encouraged me for the rest of the week.

Not only is the Bible relevant and reliable, but it also has a great deal of commonality with us. It is written about people just like you and me, and their relationship, or lack of it, with God. In James 5:17 we read,

> Elijah was a man just like us. He prayed earnestly that it would not rain, and it did not rain on the land for three and a half years.

The Bible does not paint a picture of men who were morally perfect and followed God naturally as if they were among the spiritual elite. David, Moses, Peter, and Paul all had faults, yet they loved God. Jesus, the central figure of the Bible, understands what we as men and women go through. Hebrews 4:15 tells us,

> For we do not have a high priest who is unable to sympathize with our weaknesses, but we have one who has been tempted in every way, just as we are—yet was without sin.

Think about this a moment. If I were to write a love letter to my wife, I would not send it to someone I do not know and who does not know me. That would be foolish and do no one any good. Instead, I would make sure the letter was sent to my wife at our common address.

God is no different. He has written His love letter to us— the Bible—and has sent it to us in a form that is common to us all, a form that allows all of us to relate to it, if we will.

Lastly, we have the Bible in our language. In the United States we have no excuse for not reading the Bible. Most of us have at least one Bible in our home. Unfortunately, this is probably one of the reasons why we take the Bible for granted and do not memorize, meditate, and study it. We take it for granted because it is so available, and we do not realize the power we have in God's Word.

Now that we have seen how important God's Word is, we can look at different methods of studying the Bible. This is not meant to be an exhaustive list or a legalistic command that you must study the Bible this way; it is simply a list of ideas to help get you started studying God's Word.

1. **Outline Studies.** These studies take a verse, paragraph, chapter, or book and look at its content. This can be done in one of several ways:
   a. Outline the section of Scripture being studied, then make a list of personal observations, questions, and ideas of how to apply the Scripture to everyday life.
   b. Do an overview study, read through the entire book, and compile a list of the major topics dealt with in the book. Then read more about those topics in a concordance and Bible dictionary.

2. **Topical Study.** Take a word, doctrine, or topic and look up all the places it is used in Scripture. Then draw conclusions from your research.

3. **Biographical Method.** This involves reading all of the Scriptures that relate to a particular person in the Bible. As you study and observe a person's life, look for what lessons you can learn from his or her life.

4. **Bible Memorization.** Psalm 119:11 says, "I have hidden your word in my heart that I may not sin against you." Memorizing verses or passages of Scripture is an excellent way of putting God's Word in our hearts and studying the Bible.

For more information, see *The Navigator Bible Study Handbook*, published by Navpress, or *How to Study the Bible,* by James Braga, published by Multnomah press.

In John 5:39–40 Jesus said of the Pharisees,

> You diligently study the Scriptures because you think that by them you possess eternal life. These are the Scriptures that testify about me, yet you refuse to come to me to have life.

Jesus showed us here that studying the Scriptures in and of themselves is not beneficial. The purpose of studying the Bible is to draw closer to Jesus Christ. Paul also talked about this in II Timothy 3:6–9, especially verse 7:

> Always learning but never able to acknowledge the truth.

Knowledge is not our goal, winning an argument about Scripture is not our goal, fulfilling our duty is not our goal. Knowing Christ better is our goal. With that as our goal, we take the knowledge we gain and integrate it into our personal decisions and actions, and thereby become more Christ-like. Application of Scripture to life is the point of Bible study. As we apply Scripture, we will see growth in our Christian walk.

Studying the Bible produces many results. One of them is wisdom. Psalm 119:98–100 says,

> Your commands make me wiser than my enemies, for they are ever with me. I have more insight than all my teachers, for I meditate on your statutes. I have more understanding than the elders, for I obey your precepts.

This verse came home to me when my first son was born. Nervousness filled my heart as the new responsibility of being a parent made me realize how unprepared I was for the job. As I read through the book of Proverbs and meditated on the passages that dealt with being a father, I gradually became more confident in my role of father. God had given commands, insights, and understanding in His Word about fathering that went beyond my own limited knowledge of parenthood. As the Psalmist said, God's commands has made me wiser.

Another result of studying the Bible is that of learning how to be a better Christian on the job. As a physician's assistant,

I'm currently studying the healing miracles of Christ. In the book of Matthew we read about the following miracle:

> A man with leprosy came and knelt before him and said, "Lord, if you are willing, you can make me clean." Jesus reached out his hand and touched the man. "I am willing," he said. "Be clean!" Immediately he was cured of the leprosy (Matthew 8:1–3).

As I looked at this passage and at the passages in the other gospels that talk about this miracle (Luke 5:12–16 and Mark 1:40–45), two main points stood out. Both of them convicted me and showed me how I could be a better physician's assistant. First, the Lord looked upon this man with compassion. I had to ask myself, Do I look upon my patients with compassion or as just another person I have to see to get through the day? Jesus showed me through Scripture that to be a better physician's assistant I need to have more compassion.

Second, Jesus healed more than the man's physical ailment. Jesus touched the *man*, something that no one in their right mind would have done in that day. It broke tradition and all of the rules of Jewish cleanliness. This man had not been touched in a meaningful way since he had been diagnosed with leprosy. No hugs, no handshakes, no arm around the shoulder, no pat on the back. This lack of physical touching had to cause emotional damage, and Jesus' gesture of reaching out and touching him was the healing of that damage. Jesus showed me by this that I needed to look deeper than just the physical manifestations of my patients' diseases. I also need to look at the social and emotional needs they have.

God's Word has something to say to us today. I challenge you, if you really want to see what the Bible has to say and the benefits it has to offer, to try reading and studying it for yourself—it is the only way you will know the truth for sure.

With all these benefits, why don't men believe what it says and in the One to Whom it points? There are five different reasons. First, II Corinthians 4:3–4 says that Satan has blinded men spiritually. Second, there are those who are unfamiliar with true Christianity and feel that Christians are close-minded and out of touch with reality. The third reason is the pride of man and the idea that man wants to run his life rather than give control to Jesus. Fourth, in today's moral climate we are seeking temporary gratification of sinful desires rather than seeking to know God. And fifth, there is a fear and resentment of God that has been caused by ignorance of Who God is and what He is really like.

I believe that more people would accept Christ and the Bible if they understood that there is strong evidence for their faith. So, what do we do? We have the answer—Jesus Christ. If we want to introduce Him to those who are asking the questions and trying to live life, we must do two things: (1) Study God's Word until we become convinced spiritually, mentally, and emotionally that the Bible is the inspired Word of God and that Jesus is the central figure of the book, as well as the answer for all of man's dilemmas. We need to study the Bible's history, geography, times, characters, doctrines, themes, its affect on people, and most importantly how we can know Jesus Christ more personally. (2) We need to share it at work, school, home, church, and anywhere else we can, praying for wisdom, strength, and spiritual insight as opportunities arise in the lives of those we are trying to reach or counsel with God's Word. One thing is certain: If we never read it, God cannot speak to us through it.

Questions for Chapter 4

1. What is the primary source of God's communication with us?

2. Why might a person be motivated to say that the Bible is irrelevant?

3. Read John 5:39–40. According to this passage, is it possible to read the Bible and miss its primary message? What is the primary message or theme of the Bible?

4. What should be our intent and our goal when we study the Bible? How will that affect us at home, at work and in the marketplace?

5. Name reasons men and women do not believe what the Bible says. Is there anything we can do to help them understand the life that Jesus offers?

CHAPTER 5

People

One day as I was driving from Fort Bragg to my mom and dad's home in Ohio, a truck that belonged to a major trucking company passed me. I noticed it had a bumper sticker that read, "People Are Our Driving Force."

If God were to have a bumper sticker, I think it would say the same thing. Chuck Swindoll states in his book, *Growing Deep,* that only two things are eternal—God's Word and His people. Jesus' purpose in coming to earth, dwelling among men, teaching His disciples, suffering on the cross, rising from the dead and ascending to heaven, and interceding for us at the throne of God the Father has been to save people! If we are to be Christ-like, then we also should have a people-focus. Jesus declared,

> "I am the true vine, and my Father is the gardener. He cuts off every branch in me that bears no fruit, while every branch that bears fruit he prunes so that it will be even more fruitful. You are already clean because of the word I have spoken to you. Remain in me, and I will remain in you. No

branch can bear fruit by itself; it must remain in the vine. Neither can you bear fruit unless you remain in me. I am the vine; you are the branches. If a man remains in me and I in him, he will bear much fruit; apart from me you can do nothing." (John 15:1–5)

In this passage, God the Father is the gardener; Jesus is the vine, you and I, as Christians, are the branches. The fruit stands for two things: (1) the fruit of the Spirit; and (2) those we help to walk faithfully with Jesus Christ.

There are two very important points in these words of Jesus. First, if we are not connected to Jesus as a branch is to a vine and do not have a personal relationship with Him, we cannot bear fruit of any kind. Second, we are connected at both ends, to Christ on one end and to the fruit (or people) at the other end. Christ is at one end as our power source. The other end consists of those we are helping to follow Jesus. We are the go-between from Jesus to other people. We are His ambassadors, as II Corinthians 5:20–21 says:

> We are therefore Christ's ambassadors, as though God were making his appeal through us. We implore you on Christ's behalf: Be reconciled to God. God made him who had no sin to be sin for us, so that in him we might be-come the righteousness of God.

During my first several years in the military I traveled to several foreign countries and many states throughout our country. As a member of the United States Armed Forces, I was a representative of what the Army stood for to all who came in contact with me. I was an ambassador, so to speak, for the United States Army. If I was good and behaved properly, I represented well the organization I belonged to. Because of my good actions, people saw the organization in a good light. Conversely, if I acted poorly, the Army was viewed in a bad light. The Army had not changed its policies or its traditions or the people in charge. It was the same Army, yet it was viewed two different ways based upon my lifestyle and behavior.

This is true of Christianity. We represent Jesus to the people around us. He is God and therefore does not change. The Bible says that He is the same yesterday, today, and always. Yet how people view Jesus changes daily and to a large extent depends upon the way we act as Christians. You can divide all of the people of the world into two groups—those who do not know Jesus as Lord and those who do.

Let's look at the first group. God has chosen to reach the lost through those of us who are followers of Him. He wants people to see the relationship we have with His Son and to desire that they might have that same relationship. Would someone at our workplace want to come to Jesus because of our relationship with God?

This idea of reaching out to others and trying to reach them with Jesus is not an option. Some people think that because they are not good at sharing Jesus with others, or are uncomfortable doing it, or are better at sweeping the church or taking flowers to the sick or singing in the church choir God relieves them of this responsibility. This is not so! Others use the excuse, "That is the pastor's job," to get out of sharing their faith with others. This also is not true! I struggle sometimes because I'm introverted; however, one of the last things—and, therefore, one of the most important things—Jesus said to His disciples before He ascended into heaven was,

> "All authority in heaven and on earth has been given to me. Therefore go and make disciples of all nations, baptizing them in the name of the Father and of the Son and of the Holy Spirit, and teaching them to obey everything I have commanded you. And surely I am with you always, to the very end of the age." (Matthew 28:18–20)

Jesus did not tell those who are comfortable witnessing to go make disciples, nor did He tell just those who are gifted with people skills and evangelism. The command was given to *all* of His disciples, and He expected all of them to participate. By implication He expects all of us as His disciples to do it as well.

Please do not misunderstand what I have said. Not everyone is called to be an evangelist like Billy Graham and set up meetings; not everyone is called to pass out tracts about Jesus on the street corner or go door-to-door trying to win converts. We still desperately need people with servant's hearts that will sweep the church and take flowers to the ill. The point is that all Christians need to share their faith with the people around them—co-workers, neighbors, family, and friends, regardless of what else we do for the church. The following story illustrates this point well.

Now it came to pass that a group existed who called themselves fishermen. And lo, there were many fish in the waters all around. In fact, the whole area was surrounded by streams and lakes filled with fish. And the fish were hungry.

Week after week, month after month, and year after year those who called themselves fishermen met in meetings and talked about their call to go about fishing.

Continually they searched for new and better methods of fishing. They sponsored costly nationwide and worldwide congresses to discuss fishing and to promote fishing and hear all about the ways of fishing, such as the new fishing equipment, fish calls, and whether a new bait was discovered.

These fishermen built large beautiful buildings called fishing headquarters. The plea was that everyone should be a fisherman and every fisherman should fish. One thing they did not do, however: they did not fish.

All the fishermen seemed to agree that what was needed was a board which could challenge fishermen to be faithful in fishing. The board was formed by those who had great vision and courage to speak about fishing, to define fishing, and to promote the idea of fishing in faraway streams and lakes where many other fish of different colors lived.

Large, elaborate, and expensive training centers were built whose purpose was to teach fishermen how to fish. Those who taught had doctorates in fishology. But the teachers did not fish, they only taught fishing.

Some spent much time on study and travel to learn the history of fishing and to see far away places where the founding fathers did great fishing in the centuries past. They lauded the faithful fishermen of years before who handed down the idea of fishing.

Many who felt the call to be fishermen responded. They were commissioned and sent to fish. And they went off to foreign lands…to teach fishing. Now it is true that many of the fishermen sacrificed and put up with all kinds of difficulties. Some lived near the water and bore the smell of dead fish everyday. They received the ridicule of some who made fun of their fishermen's clubs. They anguished over those who were not committed enough to attend the weekly meeting to talk about fishing. After all, were they not following the master who said, 'Follow me and I will make you fishers of men'?

Imagine how hurt some were when one day a person suggested that those who did not catch fish were really not fishermen, no matter how much they claimed to be. Yet it did sound correct. Is a person a fisherman if year after year he/she never catches a fish? Is one following if he/she isn't fishing?

The question we must ask ourselves is, Are we true fisherman?

When I first became a Christian and heard words like "evangelism," "church growth seminars," and "sharing your faith," I immediately thought of either going door-to-door or standing in a mall with questionnaires and tracts. As I thought of these things, I felt anxious because I'm not good at initiating conversations with someone I do not know. It was not until I joined The Navigators and watched men of God simply share their lives and faith with others that I recognized that, though going door-to-door and handing out questionnaires are good for planting seeds and witnessing, there was another way I was more suited to. These men practiced what I call "relational evangelism."

They would meet people at work, at sports clubs, at neighborhood outings, or any place where they came in contact with people. They would become your friend—and I use that term in a true sense. They would get to know you, help you with your car when it needed a tune-up, or help you with a personal problem. As they became your friend and tried to show you brotherly love, they would share Scripture, what their faith meant to them, or maybe answers to prayers. When your friendship developed to the place where they felt ready to share Jesus Christ with you, they did so. And whether or not you accepted Jesus at that time, they continued to be your friend. They were not pushy and they did not flaunt their faith. Neither did they hide it or back away from their convictions. Their lives were true to the words they spoke. Their "witnessing" was no longer an idea that they shared with you or something that was intangible and unable to be seen. Instead, it was a lifestyle that you could see, touch, feel, and relate to. These men—Dave, Tom, Larry, Dennis, Scott, Gary, John, Mike, Pete, Bill, Mark, Bud, Vern, Phil, and many more—changed my thinking about "witnessing" and in the process relieved many of the fears I had because of my misconceptions. Let me show you what I mean.

First, I thought that because I'm an introvert (both self-admitted and proven by every personality/psychological test I have ever taken) I would be unable to relate to people well enough to get the good news about Jesus across to them. I thought that my personality, my personhood, would not be accepted by people, and, therefore, they would reject Jesus too. The fallacy of that thinking is that God is the Creator of personality. He has the perfect personality, one that is capable of relating to anyone. That same God lives in me, and as I submit to Him and become like Him, I will be able to relate to others in a way that allows Jesus to come across. I can no longer refuse to talk to someone because of the excuse that I do not relate well to people because I am an introvert. God lives in me, and He can relate to anyone *through* anyone if we are faithful and available to Him.

Second, another fear I had as I attempted to share my faith was that I would not be able to answer all the questions or defend the gospel against the arguments of people. Look at John 1:43–46 for the solution to this. Jesus called Philip to follow Him. Philip wanted Nathaniel to come, but Nathaniel resisted and argued that nothing good could come from Nazareth; the Messiah was not to come from Nazareth. Finally Philip stopped arguing and simply told Nathaniel to come and see Jesus. The answer is that simple. People can argue theology, they can argue philosophy, but if you show them Jesus, the arguing ends.

How do we do this practically? Let me illustrate. I was witnessing to a friend once who did not believe in God. After I shared the gospel he asked some questions I could not answer to his satisfaction, questions such as, Why does evil happen if God is good? Why does God say you have to come only through Jesus and not through Buddha, Mohammed, or others? How is the Bible, a book that is written by men, the Word of God? We discussed much and agreed little. *The only thing he could not refute was what Jesus had done in my life.*

The third fear I had was that the people I shared with would not want to hear about Jesus and would see my sharing the gospel with them as a pushy, unloving act; or that they would think I was trying to force something on them; or that as I pointed out that they were sinners, they would feel unloved by me. What wrong thinking! Jesus told the parable of a pearl merchant who sold everything he owned to buy the best pearl he had ever seen. The implication of the parable is that the pearl was valuable beyond all that the pearl merchant possessed, so he sold everything he had in order to acquire that pearl.

We as Christians have a relationship with Christ, something that is more valuable than anything we or the world can imagine. The most loving thing I can do is share this relationship with someone. If you were to give me one-half of your wealth because you cared for me, I would call you generous and loving. Why should I see a person who is trying to share Jesus with someone any differently? The most loving act someone can do for another is to introduce them to Jesus.

The fourth and last fear I will share with you is the fear of failure. I was afraid that if those I shared Christ with did not come to accept Jesus into their hearts, I was a failure. If my ministry did not have lots of people, I would be seen as a failure. Look at Jesus: He taught the multitudes, touched and healed many, trained the twelve, but He invested His life in three men. More people does not necessarily mean success. As one brother told me, the depth of our walk with Jesus the breadth of our ministry are our responsibility; the number of people He brings to our sphere of influence is His responsibility.

The beauty of relational evangelism is that there are principles involved but no methods or step-by-step procedures. People are valued as people. The Christian is free to be himself and share Christ as he feels God leading him and as God uses that person's uniqueness, individuality, and style to reach people no one else could reach. The non-Christian being witnessed to does not feel as if he is a project or a duty fulfilled by the one witnessing to him. The principles are also simple and easy to remember. The first and second principles come from I Peter 3:15:

> But in your hearts set apart Christ as Lord. Always be prepared to give an answer to everyone who asks you to give the reason for the hope that you have. But do this with gentleness and respect.

First, set apart Jesus in your hearts as Lord—seek God, *seek God, SEEK GOD.* You cannot give to someone something you do not have, nor can you tell another about someone you do not know yourself. As you seek to know Christ, God will place people in your life to influence for Him.

Second, always be prepared with an answer. Sit down with a mature Christian and develop your testimony, then share it with some close Christian friends for their critique and evaluation. (This calls for honesty and a thick skin!) Now you have an answer for those who ask you about your hope.

Third, when the opportunity to share Jesus with someone presents itself, do it gently and with respect for that person. Telling someone he is a sinner and needs a Savior can cause some hard feelings if it is done harshly and without love. Remember that the goal is to win the person to Jesus, not to win an argument or theological debate.

Last and most important, pray before, during, and after sharing Christ with someone.

Let's turn our attention now to the second group of people—those who already know the Lord. As a person becomes a Christian, he enters a relationship not only with Jesus Christ but also with those who have already accepted Christ. Everyone who is a Christian is in the body of Christ, and the way we relate to and treat each other is how we treat Christ. I do not understand how this happens or how it all works, but it does.

Lest you think I'm over-stating this, let's look several places in Scripture.

> "When the Son of Man comes in his glory, and all the angels with him, he will sit on this throne in heavenly glory. All the nations will be gathered before him, and he will separate the people one from another as a shepherd separates the sheep from the goats. He will put the sheep on his right and the goats on his left.
>
> "Then the King will say to those on his right, 'Come, you who are blessed by my Father; take your inheritance, the

kingdom prepared for you since the creation of the world. For I was hungry and you gave me something to eat, I was thirsty and you gave me something to drink, I was a stranger and you invited me in, I needed clothes and you clothed me, I was sick and you looked after me, I was in prison and you came to visit me.'

"Then the righteous will answer him, 'Lord, when did we see you hungry and feed you, or thirsty and give you something to drink? When did we see you a stranger and invite you in, or needing clothes and clothe you? When did we see you sick or in prison and go visit you?'

"The King will reply, 'I tell you the truth, whatever you did for one of the least of these brothers of mine, you did for me.'

"Then he will say to those on his left, 'Depart from me, you who are cursed, into the eternal fire prepared for the devil and his angels. For I was hungry and you gave me nothing to eat, I was thirsty and you gave me nothing to drink, I was a stranger and you did not invite me in, I needed clothes and you did not clothe me, I was sick and in prison and you did not look after me.'

"They also will answer, 'Lord, when did we see you hungry or thirsty or a stranger or needing clothes or sick or in prison, and did not help you?'

"He will reply, 'I tell you the truth, whatever you did not do for one of the least of these, you did not do for me.'

"Then they will go away to eternal punishment, but the righteous to eternal life." (Matthew 25:31–46)

The focus of these words of Christ is the judgment that we all will face. Notice the determining factor of how we will be judged—how we treat others. Christianity and loving others are synonymous in God's eyes. He said,

By this all men will know that you are my disciples, if you love one another. (John 13:35)

Paul's experience on the road to Damascus is another example of this. Jesus had never been persecuted by Paul directly; only the Christians in Jerusalem had suffered at his hands. Yet, when Jesus confronted him, He said, "Why do you persecute Me?" He did not ask, "Why do you persecute My followers?" There is a mystical/spiritual and intimate union between Jesus and those who truly follow Him. As we do disservice to those who follow Jesus, we do disservice to Jesus. As we ignore the needs and personhood of fellow Christians, we ignore Christ. On the other hand, as we serve and love those who belong to Jesus, we love and serve Him. As we get to know those who belong to Jesus, we get to know Him.

The question now is, How do I love people, and am I willing to love them? Jesus is our example, and as I look at the way He loved others, I see four characteristics of love. First, His love was accepting. He accepted others as they were and where they were. The disciples with all of their faults, the man with leprosy, the Roman centurion, the paralytic, the tax collectors and sinners, the Canaanite woman, the crowds, the rich young ruler, Mary and Martha, Nicodemus, Zacchaeus, the Samaritan woman at the well, the prostitute—all were accepted by Christ. Nowhere in Scripture is there a recorded incident of Christ turning someone away, even though many rejected or turned away from Him. It did not matter what their race, religion, background, sin, gender, or nationality was: He accepted them. Blind, sighted, rich, poor, sick or well, He saw each individual as a unique person created in God's image, and that person was valuable and in need of His love. There is certainly a need for that outlook today.

There are two times in my life that stand out above all others as times when I felt accepted for who I was. The first time was a joyous event. It was when my wife accepted my proposal of marriage. I had been praying for five years that God would provide a soul mate for me, and that He did wonderfully. The second time occurred earlier in my life when everything seemed upside down. I had been deeply hurt by people very close to me and was reeling with the pain. A wonderful Christian couple, Scott and Trish, took me into their family. I could come over any time, night or day, call when I needed to talk, and cry when I needed to cry, without being made to feel like a second-rate Christian. They involved me in family activities and ministered to me from God's Word. This required Scott and Trish to be available, and that is the second principle of loving others that Christ exhibited—availability.

Nicodemus came to Jesus at night and Jesus spent time with him; mothers brought their children to Him and He blessed them; blind men called out to Him for mercy and He healed them. When He tried to get away from the crowds to teach His disciples, the crowds would show up unexpectedly and He would teach them. He was available to people because He loved them. Being available to someone is giving them the most precious commodity that you have—*time*. You can make more money, get a new job, rebuild a business, but one thing you cannot do is create more time.

On the days when I can come home for lunch the first question my oldest son and daughter ask is, "Do you have to go back to work today, Daddy?" What they are really asking is how much time they have with me: "How available are you today, Daddy?"

Exactly how available are we? On those all-too rare occasions when I say I do not have to go back to work, their faces light up and they get excited, because they know I'll be able to spend more time with them. Adults are no different. They too want to spend time with those who accept and love them.

The third precept we see as we study Christ's type of love for others is *action*. He acted on the behalf of other people. He taught, healed, called, cast out demons, fed the five thousand, touched, prayed, explained Scripture, blessed, and ultimately sacrificed His life on the cross. All of those words are action words. One of the most poignant instances of Christ taking action took place when He washed the feet of the disciples in John 13:1–17. On the night of His betrayal, when His heart was heavy because of the upcoming events of His last night on earth, the God of the universe took the place of the lowest household servant and washed the disciples' feet. How much more should we serve others with our acts?

The old adage that actions speak louder than words is applicable here. I can tell my wife that I love her, but unless I help with the children at bedtime, take care of the little things around the house that she wants done, hug her and do special little things for her, my words are hollow. Similarly, if I do not meet the needs of those in my local church, how true are my words that I love the body of Christ?

Lastly comes the idea of accountability. What do I mean by accountability? I mean holding someone responsible for their actions or lack of actions in relation to their daily walk. This involves encouraging people when they're doing well in their Christian walk, as well as pointing out sin and condemning it when we see it in those we love. Christ did this well, and one of the best examples of His both encouraging and condemning sin is found in Mark 8:27–38 in reference to Peter:

> Jesus and his disciples went on to the villages around Caesarea Philippi. On the way he asked them, "Who do people say I am?"
>
> They replied, "Some say John the Baptist; others say Elijah; and still others, one of the prophets."
>
> "But what about you," he asked. "Who do you say I am?"
>
> Peter answered, "You are the Christ." Jesus warned them not to tell anyone about him. He then began to teach them that the Son of Man must suffer many things and be rejected by the elders, chief priests and teachers of the law, and that he must be killed and after three days rise again. He spoke plainly about this, and Peter took him aside and began to rebuke him.
>
> But when Jesus turned and looked at his disciples, he rebuked Peter. "Get behind me, Satan!" he said. "You do not have in mind the things of God, but the things of men."

Then he called the crowd to him along with his disciples and said: "If anyone would come after me, he must deny himself and take up his cross and follow me. For whoever wants to save his life will lose it, but whoever loses his life for me and for the gospel will save it. What good is it for a man to gain the whole world, yet forfeit his soul? Or what can a man give in exchange for his soul? If anyone is ashamed of me and my words in this adulterous and sinful generation, the Son of Man will be ashamed of him when he comes in his Father's glory with the holy angels."

We know from other accounts of this event that Jesus praised Peter for his answer that Jesus was the Christ, and then moments later rebuked him, saying, "Get behind me, Satan." Jesus was liberal with encouragement and praise, and forthright and honest when confronting sin. We should be the same.

Just a reminder here. Remember that your family is made of people no different from those you try to witness to or have fellowship with. Satan attacks the family unit, and he will do whatever he can to destroy it, including making someone so busy evangelizing or ministering to God's people that their own family's needs go unmet. I Timothy 5:8 points out,

If anyone does not provide for his relatives, and especially for his immediate family, he has denied the faith and is worse than an unbeliever.

While the context of this passage is providing for a family's physical needs, I am sure that the principle applies to providing for your family spiritually and emotionally as well. Our spouses and children need love from us daily.

People are the most precious commodity we have. We need to take time to experience them, love them, cherish them, and serve them as Jesus did.

Questions for Chapter 5

1. Read John 15:1–5. What does Jesus mean when He commands us to remain in Him? When we choose to disobey His command, what are the consequences?

2. Why is the way we live when we are not in church such an integral part of our Christian identity?

3. Read Matthew 25:31–46. What is the standard that Jesus uses in this passage to distinguish the righteous from the unrighteous? Does this mean you can earn or work your way into heaven?

4. Who are we really serving when we serve one another?

--------- CHAPTER 6 ---------

Purity and Obedience

Recently I visited with a friend who had just put a water filtering system on the faucet of his kitchen sink. Before installing the filtering system, he could not drink the water because he did not like its taste with all the added chemicals—chlorine, fluoride, etc. However, once the water was purified he was pleased with the way it tasted and said it was good to taste just plain water.

Just as my friend desired and enjoyed pure water, so God desires pure Christians—Christians with the impurities removed. This is one of the hard, yet crucial, aspects of the Christian life. If you add water or alcohol to gasoline, the gas still looks like gas, smells like gas, pours like gas, and goes into your tank like gas. Yet when your car is started and begins to use the impure form of gasoline, your engine's power, performance, and efficiency are decreased. The amount of impurities added to the gasoline determines whether any damage has been done and whether that damage is major or minor.

The same is true of Christianity. The more impurities—for example, rebellion, pride, materialism, self, worldly perspectives—added to our Christian life, the less powerful and effective our Christian life will be. The Apostle Paul knew this, and that is why he prayed for the Philippians:

> So that you may be able to discern what is best and may be pure and blameless until the day of Christ, filled with the fruit of righteousness that comes through Jesus Christ—to the glory and praise of God. (Philippians 1:10–11)

Among Christians today you hear people say they want to know God, to see God, and to experience God, yet they say little about purity. Christ said, however:

> "Blessed are the pure in heart, for they will see God." (Matthew 5:8)

Perhaps if we focused on purity as we sought God, our knowing, seeing, and experiencing God would be more consistent. The question now is, How do I live a life that is pure? Purity and obedience are the two sides of the same coin—purity is God's part and obedience is our part. Let us look at this coin a little closer.

We will begin with God's part. Our purity is based upon what Jesus did at the cross. When we accepted Christ as our personal Savior and wholeheartedly believed that He died on the cross for our sins, we became pure in God's eyes. His blood purified us from all our sins—rebellion, pride, and our carnal human nature. God sees us as pure from that point forward. If you are like me, you are probably wondering, If this is true, why do I keep on sinning? When I do sin, does God still see me as pure? How can I be seen as pure by God if I do not feel pure? These are all good questions and deserve Biblical answers. Let's look at three passages that will lead us to the answers.

First, the account given in Numbers 21:4–9 took place after the people of Israel received the Ten Commandments. They were traveling through the wilderness on their way to the Promised Land. Let's see what happened:

They traveled from Mount Hor along the route to the Red Sea, to go around Edom. But the people grew impatient on the way; they spoke against God and against Moses, and said, "Why have you brought us up out of Egypt to die in the desert? There is no bread! There is no water! And we detest this miserable food!"

Then the Lord sent venomous snakes among them; they bit the people and many Israelites died. The people came to Moses and said, "We sinned when we spoke against the Lord and against you. Pray that the Lord will take the snakes away from us." So Moses prayed for the people. The Lord said to Moses, "Make a snake and put it up on a pole; anyone who is bitten can look at it and live." So Moses made a bronze snake and put it up on a pole. Then when anyone was bitten by a snake and looked at the bronze snake, he lived.

Let's compare this episode of the Israelites to society today. First, the Israelites were in a state of rebellion and spoke against God and their spiritual leaders. Mankind today is for the most part in a state of rebellion and curses God and godly men.

Second, the Israelites complained that God was not meeting their basic needs; we do the same today.

Third, God allowed the venomous snakes to bite the people, infecting them with poison and killing many of them. God allows sin's venom to infect us, and many people now are dying spiritually as a result.

Fourth, God provided a way for the Israelites to be healed—cleansed from the poison of the snakes and given a new life. He provides a way for us to be healed—purified of sin's devastating effects and begin life anew. God's provided way for the Israelites was to look at a pole with a snake on it and, believing God's Word and looking at the snake, they would be healed and cleansed from the venom. God's provided way for us today is to look at the cross and believe what God says about it and be cleansed from sin's venom. As Jesus said in John 3:14–15:

> "Just as Moses lifted up the snake in the desert, so the Son of Man must be lifted up, that everyone who believes in him may have eternal life."

A second Scripture confirms that as we look at the cross, we become pure and righteous in God's eyes, because He trades Jesus' perfection and purity for our imperfection and sin. In II Corinthians 5:21 we read,

> God made him who had no sin to be sin for us, so that in him we might become the righteousness of God.

Here are the answers to our questions:

1. *If God sees me as pure why do I keep on sinning?* God sees me pure from the moment I accept Him and substitutes Jesus' righteousness for my sin, but this does not remove my sinful human nature—that will take place when I get to heaven.
2. *If I do sin, does God still see me as pure?* Yes, His righteousness was given to us forever. He is true to His word and He will not take our purity away.
3. *How can I be seen by God as pure when I do not feel pure?* We must not allow our feelings to determine our thinking when those feelings are contrary to God's Word. Feelings, while they can be real, are not always accurate. God's Word is always accurate.

As I said before, God's part is our purity in His sight. God erases our sin by the cross of Christ and makes us pure. This does not free us to sin without consequence, or to sin at will, since no matter what we do we are seen as pure by God. Rather, it frees us from the pressure of performing for God, Who would rather have us know and walk with Him than observe religious duties. We are given purity by God's grace when we accept Jesus.

Now, let us look at our part—obedience, the practical side
of purity. It is interesting to look at all of the metaphors that
are used in showing the relationship of Jesus to Christians. We
are the body, He is the Head; we are the sheep, He is the
Shepherd; we are the servants, He is the Master; we are the children, He is the Father; we are the bride, He is the Bridegroom;
we are the patient, He is the Great Physician. In every case we
are in the submissive role. This is not by accident, because
before we can be obedient, we must acknowledge, submit to,
listen to, and wait for the One who leads us.

Submission has become an ugly word in our society. We
are a world of free and independent thinkers, in charge and in
control of our situations and lives—or so we think. We have
rights and privileges that are owed to us, and we are strong and
powerful and able to accomplish what we set our minds to. It
is a world full of macho Marlboro men who are setting the
standards, and Virginia Slims women who have come a long
way from what God intended. Our pride and ego have eagerly
eaten up these types of lies that the world has fed us. The idea
that submission is a bad word, even an evil word, is one of the
lies. We must recognize this attitude as a lie and learn to submit to God. To submit to God, we must learn to see Him as He
really is, as Scripture portrays Him, and not as we have pic-
tured Him through preconceived and prejudicial notions. Our
misunderstanding of Biblical faith and God's grace gives us an
unbiblical view of God and thus keeps us from submitting to
Him as we should.

Given this premise—that our view of God affects the way
we relate to Him and the way we are able to submit to Him—
I would like to present two common views that are embraced
by people today, yet are unbiblical in their portrayal of God.

The first view is that God is a stingy old man. In 1989, during Operation Just Cause in Panama, I was stationed at
Womack Army Hospital at Fort Bragg. I was the hospital liai-
son for the 82nd Airborne Division, which meant that I helped
to track down and provide for soldiers who had been injured

during the operation as they returned from Panama to the United States and eventually to Fort Bragg.

During this time thousands of letters and cards poured in from all over the United States to show concern, love, and caring for the injured soldiers. Much of this mail was simply addressed to "any soldier." This type of mail was screened to ensure that no hate-mail or mail that could affect the psychological well-being made it to the soldier. I'll never forget listening to a young captain who was a nurse as she read a card that had the following written in it: "We hope you get well soon. We are praying for you. Remember, 'For the wages of sin is death, but the free gift of God is eternal life' (Romans 3:23)."

As the captain read the card aloud, her anger and irritation came through in her voice. She wondered how anyone could be so insensitive and send a wounded soldier a card that talked of death. She hurriedly placed the letter in the pile of letters that weren't to be forwarded to the soldiers. This young captain did not see the second half of the verse—*the free gift of God is eternal life*. She saw God as a taker, not a giver of a free gift. Our society as a whole sees God that way. Many people never come to Christ because they feel that He requires too much of them and gives them nothing in return.

Hebrews 11:6 says,

> And without faith it is impossible to please God, because anyone who comes to him must believe that he exists and that he rewards those who earnestly seek him.

God is a giver and a rewarder.

Another view of God that hampers our submission to Him is the view that He is a corporate president. This image portrays Him as a very busy God Who is involved in the monstrously important business of running the universe and has no time to sit and chat or listen to me when I pray. This makes God an impersonal, cold, uncaring character who already has enough to take care of without getting involved in people's lives. No one would want to submit to a boss, husband, or God who acted like that.

Nothing could be further from the correct view of God. God may be very busy, I do not know, but this I do know— God is personal, warm, and caring, and He wants to get involved in our lives and listen to us. John 3:16 says,

> "For God so loved the world that he gave his one and only Son, that whoever believes in him shall not perish but have eternal life."

Does that sound like the description of a God who is cold and uncaring? Consider Matthew 10:29–31:

> "Are not two sparrows sold for a penny? Yet not one of them will fall to the ground apart from the will of your Father. And even the very hairs of your head are all numbered. So do not be afraid; you are worth more than many sparrows."

Does that sound like a God who is too busy to be personal? I think not. It sounds like a God Who genuinely cares and is concerned about what is best for me! Instead of seeing God as a stingy old man or a busy corporate president, we need to see Him as He really is: a God Who is righteous (see Mark 10:18; Job 34:10; I John 2:16), just (see Romans 2:11; 9:14), and loving (I John 4:7–12; Romans 8:38–39). As we begin to see God as the gracious caring person He is, as someone Who is genuinely concerned with our well being, our spirits will long for His presence. We will approach Him humbly, with assurance, ready to submit to Jesus in obedience.

As a father of a six-year-old, four-year-old, and one-year-old, I know how important it is for kids to be able to listen if they are going to be obedient. In the midst of their rambunctious play and happy, fun-filled laughter, they are not able to hear me when I call for them to come inside or to do whatever it is I want them to do.

The same is true for us. Many times we are so taken up with our lives that we do not hear God. We long to know God, to come into His presence, and to know His will, yet our lives are filled with so much noise that we cannot hear Him. Notice how God spoke to Elijah:

> The Lord said, "Go out and stand on the mountain in the presence of the Lord, for the Lord is going about to pass by."
>
> Then a great and powerful wind tore the mountains apart and shattered the rocks before the Lord, but the Lord was not in the wind. After the wind there was an earthquake, but the Lord was not in the earthquake. After the earthquake came a fire, but the Lord was not in the fire. And after the fire came a gentle whisper. When Elijah heard it, he pulled his cloak over his face and went out and stood at the mouth of the cave. (I Kings 19:11–13)

Too often we are so taken up with our busy schedules, church activities, and noisy world that we never hear the quiet whisper of the Lord. If we cannot hear Him, we cannot obey Him either. When was the last time you heard that quiet, still voice? When was the last time you listened?

This point of listening to God came home to me personally in one of my own battles with sin. One of the hardest things for me to overcome was an addiction to pornography. I had struggled with it since I was first exposed to it as a teenager. I would sneak to a store in a town where no one knew me and buy a magazine full of the filth, lust over it, throw it away, and then feel guilty and defeated. It was not until I submitted and listened to God's Word that I was able to overcome the problem. James 5:16 says,

> Therefore confess your sins to each other and pray for each other so that you may be healed.

I had to swallow my pride and risk the rejection of those I confessed my sin to as I submitted to the above Scripture passage and obeyed God. As I became accountable to other men in this area, the victory gradually came and, praise God, it has been over ten years since I have bought a pornographic magazine.

Obedience also means waiting. Again this is something we in our society do not do well. Think of all the frustrating times you've had to wait in line at the ten-item express lane of the grocery store and the person in front of you has twenty items. Or the aggravation you feel when you are trapped in a traffic jam and are late for an appointment. We live in an instant society: instant coffee, instant tea, instant pudding, instant potatoes. We want instant everything, because we do not want to wait.

We carry this attitude over into our Christian life as well. We want instant answers to our prayers, instant maturity, instant ministry, and the presence of God the instant we want it. God will not be rushed, however. Waiting on God is probably the most important part of obedience. If we do not wait on God, we have acted in our own strength and basically told God we know better than He does. We take God off the throne and put ourselves there.

Notice what happened to King Saul when he was preparing to go to war with the Philistines:

> ...Saul remained at Gilgal, and all the troops with him were quaking with fear. He waited seven days, the time set by Samuel; but Samuel did not come to Gilgal, and Saul's men began to scatter. So he said, "Bring me the burnt offering and the fellowship offerings." And Saul offered up the burnt offering. Just as he finished making the offering, Samuel arrived, and Saul went out to greet him.
>
> "What have you done?" asked Samuel.
>
> Saul replied, "When I saw that the men were scattering, and that you did not come at the set time, and that the Philistines were assembling at Micmash, I thought, 'Now the Philistines will come down against me at Gilgal, and I have

not sought the Lord's favor. So I felt compelled to offer the burnt offering."

"You acted foolishly," Samuel said. "You have not kept the command the Lord your God gave you; if you had, he would have established your kingdom over Israel for all time. But now your kingdom will not endure; the Lord has sought out a man after his own heart and appointed him leader of his people, because you have not kept the Lord's command." (I Samuel 13:7–14)

Can you see the picture here? Saul could not go into battle until his troops were blessed by Samuel, the priest, and the appropriate sacrifices were made. Samuel was delayed and the longer he was delayed, the better prepared the enemy got and the smaller and more frightened Saul's forces got. As Saul looked at the circumstances, things got bleaker, so he was compelled to act. But if he had focused on God's power, he would have been able to wait.

How often have we looked at the circumstances, seen them as bleak, and acted in our own strength instead of waiting on God? Remember also that Saul did a good thing: he made an offering to the Lord. But it was not "the Lord's thing" or "the best thing" that he did. When we act out of our own strength, as did Saul, we rob God of the opportunity to bless and move and be supremely glorified. Obedience comes from waiting on the Lord, because as we wait on Him, He enables us to trust Him and thus to obey Him.

Look at what the following Scriptures say:

1. *Wait for the Lord*; be strong and take heart and *wait for the Lord* (Psalm 27:14).
2. We *wait* in hope for the Lord; he is our help and our shield (Psalm 33:20).
3. Be still before the Lord and *wait patiently* for him; do not fret when men succeed in their ways, when they carry out their wicked schemes (Psalm 37:7).

4. *Wait for the Lord* and keep his way. He will exalt you to inherit the land; when the wicked are cut off., you will see it (Psalm 37:34).
5. I *wait* for you, O Lord; you will answer, O Lord my God (Psalm 38:15).
6. I *wait* for your salvation, O Lord, and I follow your commands (Psalm 119:166).
7. I *wait for the Lord*, my soul waits, and in his word I put my hope. My soul waits for the Lord more than watchmen wait for the morning, more than watchmen wait for the morning (Psalm 130:5–6).

Obedience is waiting on God, and waiting on God produces obedience.

Just as God's grace and our faith in Him at our salvation are what give us Christ's purity, so too faith is the key to our obedience. Paul says in the opening comments of his letter to the Romans:

> Through him and for his name's sake, we received grace and apostleship to call people from among all the Gentiles to the obedience that comes from faith. (Romans 1:5)

Notice where Paul says the obedience comes from. It comes from our faith in Jesus. As a physician's assistant, I have many patients to whom I prescribe medicine and other types of treatments. Over the past couple of years of prescribing various treatments, I have seen that the more patients know me and trust me and place their faith in me as their health care provider, the more likely they are to be obedient in following my directions for their treatment. The same is true of Jesus. The better we know Him, the more we trust Him; the more we place our faith in Him, the more likely we are to obey Him.

So we see that God gives us Jesus' purity as we place our faith in His Son for our salvation. Then we grow in our obedience as we place our faith in Jesus, submit, listen, and wait on

Him. Our faith in Him for our salvation and our faith that enables us to obey is the same faith that gives us victory over sin, death, and the world.

———◦∞◦———

Questions for Chapter 6

1. How does God see us after we have placed our faith in Jesus Christ? Does this mean we will be without sin?
2. If we still have feelings of guilt after we have confessed our sins to God, does this mean that God has not forgiven us?

3. Read Philippians 2:5–11. What does this passage illustrate?

4. What can hinder us from submitting to God as He commands?

5. Read Psalm 37:7 and 38:15. Why is waiting on the Lord so important?

6. Read I Samuel 13:7–14. What caused Saul to sin?

CHAPTER 7

Praise and Worship

Therefore, I urge you , brothers, in view of God's mercy, to offer your bodies as living sacrifices, holy and pleasing to God—this is your spiritual act of worship. Do not conform any longer to the pattern of this world, but be transformed by the renewing of your mind. Then you will be able to test and approve what God's will is—his good, pleasing and perfect will. (Romans 12:1–2)

Have you ever noticed what gets people really excited? excited to the point where they act kind of "goofy" and yell and seem like they've gone crazy? The places I can think of that cause people to act like that are sporting events, rock or music concerts, and political rallies. When not attending these events, though, people do not get really excited.

It has been said that we live in an era in which everyone is depressed. We have technology at our fingertips that can give us information within minutes on any topic we want via the Internet. We have been to the moon and seen close-up pictures of Venus and Mars. We have the medical know-how to do heart transplants and much more.

You would think that with all of this we would be happy to be living in this day and age. But more people than ever before are seeing counselors, being placed on anti-depressants, and having problems. So in order to break the boredom and monotony, to overcome the despair, they go to professional football games or music concerts and let all of those pent-up emotions come out. They holler, raise their hands, do the wave, dance, and sing for several hours, only to return to their same lifestyle, because there's nothing in the sporting event or the concert that is lasting and able to cure their complacency and despair.

Have you ever wondered what it would be like if we got that excited about Jesus? I mean excited to the point of passion like the kind we show when we watch our favorite football team score a touchdown. The same person who on Saturday night at the concert yells at the top of his lungs to the point of losing his voice, and who jumps up and down throwing confetti all over the place and is considered perfectly normal, is looked at as odd, strange, or fanatical if he says amen when he agrees with the pastor the very next day.

As we praise God, we become focused on Him and our lives are changed. He changes us and places a new song in our hearts. Deep down in our inner person where no one but God can see, He restores us to what we were created to be, and the anger, pain, boredom, and despair are taken away. They are replaced with joy, peace, love, and hope. I do not understand how this works, and it does not always happen immediately, but it does happen.

If I could start my Christian life over again knowing then what I know now, one of the first aspects of my life that I would change would be in the area of praise and worship. Leviticus 19:23–25 commands,

> When you enter the land and plant any kind of fruit tree, regard its fruit as forbidden. For three years you are to consider it forbidden; it must not be eaten. In the fourth

year all its fruit will be holy, an offering of praise to the Lord. But in the fifth year you may eat its fruit. In this way your harvest will be increased. I am the Lord your God.

The *first* fruits of the fruit trees of Israel were praise offerings to God. I have been a Christian for close to twenty-five years now, and I am just beginning to understand, appreciate, and consider the importance of praise in my life. All too often I have been a complainer instead of a praise warrior. I had been so infiltrated by the world system that I had forgotten how to praise. Have you ever wondered why companies do not have praise departments, but they do have complaint departments? How often do you see a praise form? On most tables at restaurants across the United States there are complaint or comment cards to fill out. We have forgotten how to praise anyone or anything, especially God. Our grateful hearts have been squelched.

Reviving our thankful hearts is the first step in returning to a people who praise and worship God. How do we do this? A good illustration of how this works was when I was in the Kingdom of Saudi Arabia during Desert Shield/Storm. All the things I had grown accustomed to were suddenly no longer there. My wife and first son were still at Fort Bragg; all the love, encouragement, and help that Sue gave daily at home now came only occasionally as her letters made it to me. While we had water to drink, it was hot, and there was no ice or refrigeration available. Showers or baths were non-existent for the first week or so and for the last forty to fifty days of our deployment. The everyday, normal things—the things that I considered routine and therefore never appreciated properly prior to my departure—were suddenly and emphatically brought to my attention when they were gone. As I recalled my wife's gentle touch and loving words, both those spoken before I left and those in her letters, a new thankfulness to God for her welled up in my heart. As the memory of my seven-month-old son was kept fresh by my picture of him, again gratitude to God for the privilege of being a father gained control of my heart.

What blessings have you grown accustomed to in your daily walk with God? Do you remember that He created you and gave you life today? Does the day that you accepted Jesus and received salvation still have a place in your heart's memory bank? We are a forgetful people, no different from the Israelites of the Old Testament, who saw God deliver them from the Egyptians with plagues, miraculously rescue them through the Red Sea, provide water and food for them supernaturally, yet when faced with the giants of the Promised Land they refused to go in. They had forgotten the prior blessings and the present promises of God.

We are guilty of the same thing today. No wonder God uses the word "remember" hundreds of times in the Bible. We must constantly seek to remember and recall what God has already done for us—salvation, answers to prayer, family, friends, and much more. As we remember, our hearts will overcome the complaining spirit of our society and be resuscitated by gratitude, thus leading us to praise and worship.

As we begin to develop grateful hearts, our focus will shift to God and away from ourselves. This is the beginning of praise—God-centeredness. Before writing this chapter today, I went to a worship service where the pastor was speaking about praising and worshipping God. He had the congregation do the following exercises to make his point: first, he had everyone yell the name of their favorite hymn on the count of three. Second, he had them yell the name of the place where they accepted Christ. Both times this happened there was much noise; people's voices mixed together, but nothing was intelligible. The third time he told the congregation to call out the name of the One who died for them and saved them from their sin. When the people responded that time, it was audible and intelligible, no longer just noise. The name Jesus was heard all over that church. The response the third time was focused, just as our praise should be.

Moses put it this way in Deuteronomy 10:20–21:

> Fear the Lord your God and serve him. Hold fast to him
> and take your oaths in his name. He is your praise; he is your
> God, who performed for you those great and awesome won-
> ders you saw with your own eyes.

The focus of our praise is to be God. Look at the verses in
Romans that begin this chapter; the reason we can offer our
bodies as living sacrifices, holy and pleasing to God, is because
of the view of God's mercy. If our focus, our line of sight, our
view, our outlook, is centered and fixed on God and His mercy,
our eyes must be off our selves, our sin, and our circumstances.
As He becomes the all-consuming passion of our lives, we die
to self. This is the living sacrifice part.

Have you ever noticed this oxymoron? The words "living"
and "sacrifice" are two totally opposite concepts, yet that is how
we are to worship—sacrifice, by putting to death self, pride,
dreams, goals, rights, on the altar of a loving merciful God—
living, by receiving from God in return for our sacrifice a life
that is more beautiful and wonderful than we can imagine.

King David knew this also. In II Samuel 24 he went to a
man named Araunah and offered to buy his land so he could
build an altar and make a burnt offering to God. Araunah told
David he could have the land as a gift, but David replied,

> "No, I insist on paying you for it. I will not sacrifice to
> the Lord my God burnt offerings that cost me nothing." (II
> Samuel 24:24)

David knew that praise and worship, done in the form of
the burnt offerings in his day, required sacrifice.

Now that we have seen that praise and worship require sacrifice, let's look at some of the "living" aspects of praise and
worship. Praise and worship come in the form of singing and
dancing. Yes, I said singing and dancing. Singing is probably

one of the best-known ways to praise God, as well as one that is fun, easy to do, and can be done anytime and anywhere. The Bible is full of examples of song used in praise. It is no coincidence that the longest book of the Bible is a book of songs for worshipping and praising God.

Two of the tools that best help me to praise God are my hymnal and my cassette player. "In the Garden," "How Great Thou Art," "Holy, Holy, Holy," and many other great old hymns are fantastic ways to praise God. If you are like me and cannot sing very well and do not have any musical ability, there are hundreds of great cassette tapes by Christian artists with moving songs that promote praise and worship. My wife is tired of listening to one of the cassettes I have because I listen to it over and over again. However, the songs on that tape touch me at a deep level, and I identify with the words. This enables me to place myself before God in an attitude of praise and worship.

God enjoys praise through song also. In fact, He surrounds Himself with it. In Revelation 15:2–4 we see this:

> And I saw what looked like a sea of glass mixed with fire and, standing beside the sea, those who had been victorious over the beast and his image and over the number of his name. They held harps given them by God and sang the song of Moses the servant of God and the song of the Lamb:
> "Great and marvelous are your deeds,
> Lord God Almighty.
>   Just and true are your ways,
> King of the ages.
>   Who will not fear you, O Lord,
> and bring glory to your name?
>   For you alone are holy.
> All nations will come
>   and worship before you,
>   for your righteous acts have been revealed."

Remember, I said singing and dancing; we've dealt with the singing, so now it is time to look at the more controversial form of praise—dancing. Please do not misunderstand me here. Not all dancing is praise-worthy or worshipful or even pleasing to God. Yet, there are times when people are so excited and joyful in the Lord that they express it in dance. Again we will look at David, who danced and rejoiced as the Ark of the Covenant was returned to Jerusalem. Psalm 149:3 says,

> Let them praise his name with dancing and make music to him with tambourine and harp.

Psalm 150:4 echoes this:

> Praise him with tambourine and dancing, praise him with the strings and flute.

One of the best examples I have seen of this in today's world is on the video *Standard,* by Carmen. People praise God and dance in the aisles and at their seats as the gospel is shared in song. Praise and worship take place in singing and dancing.

Praise and worship are also weapons of spiritual warfare. There is something about praise and worship to God that sends shock waves through the spiritual realm. Our praise to God subverts Satan's causes by exposing our sin, helping us to confess our sin, and enabling us to conquer our sin through Jesus Christ.

During my training at the Army Flight Surgeon Primary Course, the other trainees and I were instructed on night vision goggles/devices. These are instruments that take the available light and magnify it so that as you wear the goggles in the night, you are able to see as clearly as if it were day. We were placed in a room that was completely dark, the walls were painted black, there were no windows, and the door was designed to keep out light.

As I stood in that room, it became very evident to me that light and darkness cannot occupy the same room at the same time. The light overcomes the darkness. With the lights completely out, a match or lighter or even the light from someone's watch stood out and images became apparent again. As we praise God and turn our focus on Him, our own sin is so contrasted to His perfection and purity that it stands out to us clearly. As we continue to praise God, the natural response for those who know Jesus is to confess their sin.

We see this occur in Scripture in Joshua 7:19. The people of Israel had just defeated Jericho and were continuing on their campaign to conquer the rest of the Promised Land by attacking the city of Ai. Their first attack on the city was disastrous, and they met defeat because a man named Achan sinned against God by keeping booty from the battle of Jericho, something God had forbidden. Notice what Joshua said as he confronted Achan,

> Then Joshua said to Achan, "My son, give glory to the Lord, the God of Israel and give him the praise. Tell me what you have done, do not hide it from me" (Joshua 7:19, emphasis added).

Joshua knew that praise and worship reveal the real God and expose our sin so that we confess it before God and others. First praise exposes our sin; then it helps us confess our sin to God; finally, it helps us conquer sin. Let me illustrate. As I said earlier, one of the areas I struggle with the most is that of lust and wanting to look at pornographic material. As a young teenager I was exposed to it and have fallen many times in my Christian walk by looking at it. God has shown me, however, that when I am in line at the mini-mall or the gas station and the *Playboy* and *Penthouse* are right on the other side of the counter begging me to buy them, if I will, by an act of my will, start singing a song of praise, He will help me turn my focus on Jesus and away from the magazines. I am enabled to walk away from the counter without buying an evil magazine. Satan's hold is broken by praise.

Another way that praise subverts Satan's tactics is by defeating pride. Psalm 95:6 says,

> Come, let us bow down in worship, let us kneel before the Lord our maker.

If we take this position in worship—bowed down and kneeling—whether physically or in our hearts, our pride will go out the window. It is hard to be proud in a bowed down and kneeling position.

Praise leads to victory in the Christian life. Look at what Paul and Silas did after being unjustly beaten, imprisoned, and placed in stocks:

> About midnight Paul and Silas were praying and singing hymns to God, and the other prisoners were listening to them. Suddenly there was such a violent earthquake that the foundations of the prison were shaken.
>
> At once all the prison doors flew open, and everybody's chains came loose. The jailer woke up, and when he saw the prison doors open, he drew his sword and was about to kill himself because he thought the prisoners had escaped. But Paul shouted, "Do not harm yourself! We are all here!"
>
> The jailer called for the lights, rushed in and fell trembling before Paul and Silas. He then brought them out and asked, "Sirs, what must I do to be saved?" (Acts 16:25–30)

If you want to talk about bad days, Paul and Silas were having one. They were doing God's work on their way to a prayer meeting when it all started. They are harassed by a demon-possessed girl, dragged into court, falsely accused, ridiculed by the crowds, stripped, flogged, and put in prison. Have you ever had days where, in spite of your good intentions and best efforts, things looked terrible? Physically Paul did not feel like praising

God, yet he knew that praising God would take his eyes off of his circumstances and help him focus on the God of the universe Who could change the course of events. God caused the earthquake, the freedom of the prisoners, and the salvation of the jailer as a result of Paul and Silas doing two things: (1) prayer, and (2) praise in the form of singing hymns. God will respond to our praise that way too.

Praise and worship are also a summons to or pursuing of Jesus. Scripture says that God inhabits the praise of His people; He lives within and His presence is in attendance when we praise Him. When I think of this idea, I picture two events in my mind. The first is that of the people of Israel in the desert, with God inhabiting the tabernacle and leading them with a cloud of smoke by day and a pillar of fire by night. There was no doubt about God's whereabouts. He was visibly there with them.

Praise and worship is getting closer to God, having Him live with you as He did with the Israelites. James put it this way,

> Come near to God and he will come near to you. (James 4:8)

The second mental picture I get is that of Moses approaching the burning bush and God telling him to take off his shoes because he stood on holy ground. (See Exodus 3.) Our praise and worship are a summons to and pursuing of God, and as we come into the presence of God, we must recognize the awesomeness of our encounter with Him and the purity of heart He asks of us. This is where the second half of James 4:8 becomes significant:

> Wash your hands, you sinners, and purify your hearts, you double-minded.

Praise and worship provide strength. Nehemiah said that the joy of the Lord is our strength. Try praising God and not being joyful at the same time; it cannot be done. Notice

Scripture does not say the happiness of the Lord is our strength. Happiness is the feeling you get when circumstances are great and things are just the way you ordered them.

Joy, on the other hand, is the confidence and trust in God that is deeply centered in your innermost being. It is that which holds you firm and is not destroyed when circumstances are terrible and very much other than what you would like. This comes from praising God and focusing on Him, as we learned earlier. That is why Paul said,

> Rejoice in the Lord always. I will say it again: Rejoice! (Philippians 4:4)

Praise enables us to focus on the Lord, and our Godly focus enables us to receive and express joy. This God-given joy cannot be overcome by circumstances. Thus the joy of our God gives us strength, and the route to that strengthening joy is praise and worship.

Praise and worship can also take on the form of shouting. Leviticus 9:24, Psalm 27:6, and Psalm 33:3 talk of shouting for joy to the Lord, as do Ezra 3:11, Psalm 66:2, and Psalm 81:1. In the revival days of early Methodism, many of the new converts to Christ were so overcome with emotion and joy that they ran up and down the aisles shouting praises to His name.

Up to this point, I have talked mainly about things we do as individuals to praise God. Reviving our attitude of gratefulness, remembering what God has done for us in the past, focusing on God, sacrificing self, singing and dancing, subverting Satan's plans by our praise, summoning God's presence, strengthening our spirit, and expressing our praise to God in shouts of triumph are all aspects of our individual worship and praise life. These take place at home where no one is present but you and God. This individual worship is the key to corporate worship, or your worship services at church.

There's an old computer term, GIGO, that means "garbage in garbage out." The reason that many of today's churches do not have vital, vibrant worship services is that the individuals who go to the services do not have vibrant, vital lives of worship at home! Corporate worship and praise during Sunday morning worship services aren't meant to entertain or rejuvenate and revitalize us (although these things often happen). Instead, the worship services should be where the joy of the Lord overflows from us in praise and worship so that the outside world will see what we have in Jesus Christ and desire it.

Also, as we participate in praise and worship as a congregation something unique happens. It is similar to what happens when an orchestra plays a beautiful piece of music: the flute has its part, the cello has its part, the kettle drum has its part, and the other instruments have their parts. As all the instruments play together, they produce wonderful music. The beautiful music is greater than the parts by themselves.

When we praise and worship together as a congregation, we each help to produce the symphony of praise that goes to God and echoes through the spiritual realm. This corporate praise and worship is also a heavenly act. Look at Revelation 4:8–11:

> Each of the four living creatures had six wings and was covered with eyes all around, even under his wings. Day and night they never stop saying: "Holy, Holy, Holy, is the Lord God Almighty, who was, and is, and is to come."
>
> Whenever the living creatures give glory, honor and thanks to him who sits on the throne and who lives for ever and ever, the twenty-four elders fall down before him who sits on the throne, and worship him who lives for ever and ever. They lay their crowns before the throne and say:
>
> "You are worthy, our Lord and God, to receive glory and honor and power, for you created all things, and by your will they were created and have their being."

As we participate in praise and worship on Sunday morning, other Christians all across the United States and the world are doing the same thing, and we're all in tune with the throne room of God where He is being praised continually. That is an awesome and glorious act of praise and worship to be a part of!

I hope that after learning about praise and worship in this chapter you will come away with the sense that it is a lifestyle and not saying a bunch of words or rote phrases. Until recently I thought of praise as difficult and hard to do because I limited it to speech: "Praise God," "Hallelujah," "Glory be to God." I felt that all I was doing was saying the same words over and over again, and, quite frankly, I got bored with it. As I went from seeing praise and worship as something I say for or to God, to seeing it as entering into intimate communion with the one who is worthy of my words and life of praise, the boredom has been replaced by a sense of God's awesomeness.

If you are like me, much of what I said in this chapter will make you uncomfortable. You may be thinking, Do I dare say amen in church? Do I dare get a Christian tape and sing with it at the top of my lungs? Do I dare weep for joy during a worship service? What will people think? What will they say? What will my spouse or children do if I act this way?

I pray for you, as well as for myself, that you may be freed from the conservative, traditional inhibitions and pride that squelch our praise and worship of God! Jesus said that if we do not praise Him the rocks and stones will. Let us praise and worship the awesome God we serve.

Questions for Chapter 7

1. Read Romans 12:1–2. What should prompt us to offer our bodies as living sacrifices? How are we to be transformed or changed?

2. What happens to Christians when they praise God? How can we develop praise to God in our own lives?

3. Why is God-centeredness the beginning of praise? What is the connection between God-centeredness and offering our bodies as living sacrifices?

4. What can we use to help us in our praise and worship?

5. How are praise and worship spiritual warfare? What does praise and worship expose?

6. What should we do when our circumstances are so bad we don't feel like engaging in praise and worship?

CHAPTER 8

Perserverance

Therefore, since we are surrounded by such a great cloud of witnesses, let us throw off everything that hinders and the sin that so easily entangles, and let us run with perseverance the race marked out for us. Let us fix our eyes on Jesus, the author and perfector of our faith, who for the joy set before him endured the cross, scorning its shame, and sat down at the right hand of the throne of God. Consider him who endured such opposition from sinful men, so that you will not grow weary and lose heart.

In your struggle against sin, you have not yet resisted to the point of shedding your blood. And you have forgotten that word of encouragement that addresses you as sons:

"My son, do not make light of the Lord's discipline, and do not lose heart when he rebukes you, because the Lord disciplines those he loves, and he punishes everyone he accepts as a son." Endure hardship as discipline; God is treating you as sons. For what son is not disciplined by his father?

If you are not disciplined (and everyone undergoes discipline), then you are illegitimate children and not true sons. Moreover, we have all had human fathers who disciplined us and we respected them for it. How much more should we submit to the Father of our spirits and live! Our fathers disciplined us for a little while as they thought best; but God disciplines us for our good, that we may share in His holiness. No discipline seems pleasant at the time, but painful.

Later on, however, it produces a harvest of righteousness and peace for those who have been trained by it. Therefore, strengthen your feeble arms and weak knees. "Make level paths for your feet," so that the lame may not be disabled, but rather healed. (Hebrews 12:1–13)

One of the best movies of our time is *Gettysburg*. It has great music, excellent actors, and gives a clear portrayal of both good and bad leadership. I have watched the movie several times, and there's one person who always stands out to me more than any other—Joshua Lawrence Chamberlain, commander of the Twentieth Maine, a battalion under General Hancock of the Union Army. In every scene in which he is portrayed his perseverance comes through. The speech he gave to the men who wanted to desert the Army, the protection he gave his brother, the compassion he had for his fallen comrades, and, most importantly, his actions on a hill called Little Round Top all show his character.

As the battle developed, it appeared that the Twentieth Maine would not be a major contender, since they were the extreme left flank of the Union Army and the main battle would be fought closer to the center of the Union's line of defense.

Colonel Chamberlain's mission was to see that the Army was not flanked by the Confederates where they could get behind Union lines. But unexpectedly the Confederates tried to do that very thing, so Colonel Chamberlain and the Twentieth Maine became the focal point of the battle in its early stages. The Confederate soldiers attacked again and again, and with each attack Colonel Chamberlain and his men repelled them.

But after hours of fighting, his men were not only wounded and tired, but out of ammunition as well. And still the rebels were preparing for another attack. Seeing no other alternative, Colonel Chamberlain gave the command to fix bayonets and led the charge with his sword.

Needless to say, the Twentieth Maine held their position, the Confederates were pushed back, and Colonel Chamberlain, having stood firm time and time again, fulfilled his mission.

The battle continued throughout the day, and 53,000 men were killed. But the Union Army won the battle because Colonel Chamberlain stood his ground. Many scholars believe that this battle was the turning point of the Civil War, which continued for two more years. During those two years Colonel Chamberlain was wounded six times and won the Congressional Medal of Honor. What takes a man from being a teacher of rhetoric and theology to winning a Medal of Honor? Discipline, dedication, hope, endurance, consistency, and courage. Or, in one word—perseverance.

Perseverance is a rare quality today. Instead of trying to work things out, people divorce. If a course of study is too hard, they change majors. If a job is unpleasant, they quit and find something easier. In our Christian walk, we do the following: The Bible's too hard for me to understand, so I will not study it. That person is too hard to talk to, so I will not witness to him. It is too hard to go against the crowd, so I'll just be quiet. That sin is too hard for me to overcome, so I'll give up and indulge in it any way.

One of the most difficult things I had to deal with in my early Christian life was staying the course in the face of opposition. No one told me that Christianity could be hard at times. I thought that after I accepted Christ as my Savior all my difficulties would go away, because God would bless me. I romanticized Christianity. We (myself in particular) tend to romanticize everything. We look at professional athletes and idolize them and say how great it would be to be able to do what they do. Yet we forget about the pain of overcoming injuries, or the continual practice, practice, practice it takes to stay on top of the game.

We see a movie like *Gettysburg* and characters like Colonel Chamberlain to whom we'd give our respect and loyalty if he were here today; we forget the hours of studying tactics, the monotony of drill and ceremonies, the ever-present pain of seeing friends die. I saw Christianity the same way. The preachers who had great faith, the "togetherness" of the person who led me to Christ and her excitement about Jesus, and the talk of God's love and blessing were all I could see. The first time major trials and temptations hit me, I floundered because I had not seen that the great faith of the people I looked up to came because they endured trials, or that God's love and blessing also come in the form of hardships to mature us. I had to learn perseverance.

I do not want you to be caught unawares as I was. Perseverance is one of the qualities we need to develop in the Christian life. We need to learn to run the race with perseverance. In order to do that, let's take a close look at Hebrews 12:1–13, the passage that appears at the beginning of this chapter.

The first thing we see is that in the race of life we're being watched. The picture the writer of Hebrews was painting was of an Olympic marathon runner who has almost completed his 26.22 miles and is running into the stadium for the final lap. All the eyes in the stadium are on him. The crowd is cheering for him to finish and win the race.

As we run the Christian race, we are being watched. The saints in heaven are looking down and cheering us on, the Christians of today are watching and encouraging us to finish and are being encouraged by us as well. Lastly, non-Christians are watching us to see if we will make it.

I have only run one marathon in my life—the 1984 Bank One Columbus, Ohio, Marathon. When I got to mile twenty-four and had only two miles to go, I wanted to get out of my body, it hurt so bad. My muscles were cramping, my knees, ankles, hips, and everything in between hurt with every jarring stride, but I did not quit. I did not quit because as I came to the last two miles of the course I turned onto Front Street, then to Broad Street for the finish. On these two streets hundreds of people line the street, clapping for you, calling out words of encouragement, and yelling to you to hang tough and not quit.

Human nature is such that we tend to try harder when we know we're being watched. Next time the sin you are most susceptible to raises its ugly head in the form of a temptation, or the trials you face make you want to quit, remember that David, Moses, Elijah, Abraham, Peter, Paul, and many more are pulling for you and cheering you on as they watch from their seats in heaven.

The second thing the writer of Hebrews tells us to do when we run is to get rid of excess baggage. The word picture here that the author is trying to get across is that of a long-distance runner in training who has strapped weights to his ankles so that he'll be able to run faster and farther on the day of the race when the weights are removed. I have never run with ankle weights, but I have run with a rucksack (a military backpack) on my back. For those of you who have done neither, it is much easier to run without the additional weight!

As we get closer to Jesus and continue to run the Christian race, God will reveal to us what we need to get rid of as we go. What is keeping you from running the Christian race effectively? What is the weight you are carrying that is causing you to trip and fall? Maybe it is something obvious—profanity, an alcohol problem, an adulterous affair. Or maybe it is something less dramatic but just as entangling, like gossip, resentment, bitterness, or a grudge against someone. What it is many times, however, is an insidious hidden passion for something that may be a good thing, in and of itself, but, because it stands between you and the Lord and prevents you from running your best for Him, it has slowed you down. The desire to be married, a successful career, even looking good in ministry—all of these are desired things, all of them are good in and of themselves, but if we focus on them instead of Jesus, they are a hindrance to us.

So, the first step is to realize we are being watched and cheered on; the second is that we are to get rid of the weights; and the third is to run the race. The world has yet to see the person who won a marathon without taking a step. Racing requires effort, it requires participating, it means being involved, it is work. Not only is it work and putting one foot in front of the other one step at a time, but we each must run *our* race.

As I write this, the 1996 Olympic trials for swimming are on TV. While the swimmers that are trying out may swim in a couple of different races, generally they each have their own special event in which they shine. That race is *their* race.

God has made us in such a way that only we can live the life given to us. Our Christian life and calling will be different from someone else's and we must run *it*—not someone else's.

The last step in learning how to persevere is the most important. We must *fix our eyes on Jesus*. At the United States Army Flight Surgeon's Primary Course there is a poster of a skier making his way down a hill covered with multiple obstacles. The caption underneath the picture says, "Obstacles are those frightful things you see when you take your eyes off your goals."

Our goal as Christians is to love the Lord with all our hearts and souls and minds. It is when we take our eyes off Jesus that we struggle with the obstacles. The rest of Hebrews 12:1–13 deals with keeping our eyes on Jesus. Let us see what it has to say.

First, we see that Jesus is the Perfector of our faith. What does it mean to us today that Jesus is the Perfector of our faith? It is like having Leonardo da Vinci paint your house, Arnold Palmer and Jack Nicklaus teaching you how to play golf, or Charles Lindbergh and Chuck Yeager giving you private pilot's lessons. When I'm defeated or discouraged because I think I should be more spiritually mature or know Jesus better, I need only to take my eyes off myself again and return my gaze to

Jesus. As I do this, I'm reminded that He is the Perfector of my Faith. That is why Paul said in his letter to Timothy,

> That is why I am suffering as I am. Yet I am not ashamed, because I know whom I have believed, and am convinced that he is able to guard what I have entrusted to him for that day. (II Timothy 1:12)

Paul had entrusted his life and everything else to Jesus, and he knew that Jesus would not let him down. We can do the same. What hope, knowing Jesus is working on us and our faith!

As we look to Christ, we also see that He is our example for endurance. He endured the cross and opposition from sinful men for us. Not only that, but God gives us endurance as well. Romans 15:5 says,

> May the God who gives endurance and encouragement give you a spirit of unity among yourselves as you follow Christ Jesus.

As an Aeromedical Physician's Assistant for the Army, I'm required to fly for four hours a month in order to stay on flight status. The reason the Army requires this is so that as a health care provider I'll better understand the stresses and demands placed upon aviators as they fly. There is no other way to do that, except to sit where they sit and do what they do when they're flying.

Jesus came to earth for the same reason. He has experienced whatever you are struggling with. He has sat where you sit and understands what you are going through. He endured the cross and the shame that went along with it so that we would not grow weary and lose heart. Keeping our eyes on Jesus reminds us of how much He loves us and how much He endured for us and puts our struggles in perspective. I haven't resisted to the point of sweating blood as Jesus did in the garden, nor have I faced the shame and the pain of the cross.

Another aspect of gazing on Christ continually is that of the opposition we will face. As you read Hebrews 12, notice the language that is used—words such as "throw off," "hinders," "entangles," "perseverance," "endured," "shame," "opposition," "struggles," "resisted," "discipline," and "hardship." The Christian life isn't for slackers, but for soldiers. From the moment we accept Jesus as our Lord and Savior, our enemy Satan puts his forces against us: doubt, discouragement, disorder, increased demands on our time, as well as all kinds of tactics to get our eyes off Christ and onto ourselves. We need to think more like soldiers. That is why Paul said in Ephesians,

> Finally, be strong in the Lord and in his mighty power. Put on the full armor of God so that you can take your stand against the devil's schemes. For our struggle is not against flesh and blood, but against the rulers, against the authorities, against the powers of this dark world and against the spiritual forces of evil in the heavenly realms. Therefore, put on the full armor of God, so that when the day of evil comes, you may be able stand your ground, and after you have done everything, to stand. Stand firm then, with the belt of truth buckled around your waist, with the breastplate of righteousness in place, and with your feet fitted with the readiness that comes from the gospel of peace.
>
> In addition to all this, take up the shield of faith, with which you can extinguish all the flaming arrows of the evil one. Take the helmet of salvation and the sword of the spirit, which is the word of God. And pray in the spirit on all occasions with all kinds of prayers and requests. With this in mind, be alert and always keep on praying for all the saints. (Ephesians 6:10–18)

We will struggle for the rest of our lives. When a young recruit enlists in the United States Army, he goes to basic training; then he goes to his advanced individual training. After these two schools, he goes to his unit of assignment where he learns his job and how to be a soldier through hands-on and on-the-job training. If you were going to face an army in battle, who would you rather face—a group of new recruits fresh out of basic or a group of well-trained soldiers? Or if you were engaged in an actual fire fight where real bullets were flying and you had two targets of opportunity, who would you choose to place in your sites—a soldier paralyzed by fear who was curled up in his foxhole, or a soldier holding his ground and returning fire?

Satan is a great tactician. He'll do everything in his power to keep the new Christian recruits just that—new recruits with no spiritual training. He will also concentrate his efforts on those who are actively engaged in the battle. Warfare, both physical and spiritual, is hard and requires perseverance.

If you are like me and like the rest of our society, you may be thinking, "Great, just great, my life is hard enough as it is. I do not need to enter another conflict. Why am I doing this? Is it worth it to stand firm in my faith?" Let me assure you, it is, and as we return our focus to Jesus, we see that. As we look at Jesus we remember what the writer of Hebrews told the people to remember:

> And you have forgotten the word of encouragement that addresses you as sons: "My son, do not make light of the Lord's discipline, and do not lose heart when he rebukes you, because the Lord disciplines those he loves, and he punishes everyone he accepts as a son."
>
> Endure hardship as discipline; God is treating you as sons. (Hebrews 12:5–7)

The first reason we see that it is worthwhile to enter the struggle and hardship is that, as we do, we are confirmed as God's children. We move into a deeper relationship with God. Secondly, we see that our hardships and our trials have purpose. Geraldo Rivera appeared once on the television show, *The Lifestyles of the Rich and Famous* and said, "I believe life is short and hard, and then you die." How sad to believe that. No direction or purpose is seen in that philosophy. Yet many today claim that as their own belief, and so they strive to live lives that have no suffering or pain and, consequently, no purpose.

The Bible says that we do have purpose and that the hardships and trials we endure have purpose too. James 1:2–4 tells us to:

> Consider it pure joy, my brothers, whenever you face trials of many kinds, because you know that the testing of your faith develops perseverance. Perseverance must finish its work so that you may be mature and complete, not lacking anything.

You see, Geraldo was right about the first two things: life is short and hard at times, but for the Christian, there is no death but maturity and completeness. For those of you who are going through a hard time right now, I encourage you to hold on and keep focusing on Jesus. Submit yourselves to what God is doing. The pain of discipline now is worth the righteousness and peace that are promised in verse eleven. The pain now trains us for the future.

As we stand firm and as we are trained by the discipline of hardship, the author of Hebrews tells us to do something that seems impossible. He says we are to make our arms and legs, that are weak and feeble, strong. How do we do that? When we are tired of holding on, when we want to give up or give in, when it seems that all our strength is gone, we are to strengthen our arms and legs! At first glance this looks like a positive-thinking, pull-yourself-up-by-the-bootstraps mentality, but it isn't. Nor is it a hold-on-no-matter-what duty that binds us to habits that are just that and nothing more.

One of the most important parts of flying is the preflight check of the aircraft. As aviators get more experience, more confidence in their ability to fly, more familiar with the aircraft, the preflight becomes more habitual. The challenge for these aviators is to guard against complacency and doing the preflight checks without really doing the preflight check. For the aviator, the preflight must never become just a habit where he looks at the aircraft but does not really see it.

In the Christian life, we must guard against that same kind of complacency. Strengthening our arms and legs isn't studying the Bible, praying, and having quiet times out of habit, where we study God's Word but do not really see the truth. We must depend on His strength, not our impulsive actions. So, if the strength to continue is His strength and not pulling yourself up by your bootstraps or continuing the good habits out of duty, how do we avail ourselves of this power and His strength? The second half of the command to strengthen our arms and legs commands, "Make level paths for your feet in order that *the lame may not be disabled but rather healed.*"

The strength we get from persevering in this life comes from the love we give to others; for example, in ministry to the lame. The lame are all around us. Not long ago a man walked into an elementary school in Scotland and killed sixteen children, a teacher, and himself. The families of those children are hurting and emotionally lame.

Broken relationships are commonplace; they leave families broken and lame. Shattered dreams and loneliness are in every community across this land, and we have the therapy they need to help them be healed instead of be disabled—the love of Christ.

Jesus knew this. In John 4 He traveled to Samaria and there met the woman at the well. The disciples went to get food while Jesus ministered to this woman. When the disciples returned, they urged Jesus to eat, but He replied,

"I have food to eat that you know nothing about."

Then his disciples said to each other, "Could someone have brought him food?"

"My food," said Jesus, "is to do the will of him who sent me and to finish his work. Do you not say, 'Four months more and then the harvest'? I tell you, open your eyes and look at the fields! They are ripe for harvest." (John 4:32–35)

Perseverance God's way—being encouraged by those in heaven cheering us on; getting rid of the extras that trip us up; running our race; and keeping our eyes focused on our Faith Perfector, Endurance Example, Encourager, Jesus Christ— brings healing to others and thereby to ourselves.

——— ⌘ ———

Questions for Chapter 8

1. Read Hebrews 12:1–13. According to verse 2, what enabled Jesus to endure the cross? What is the purpose of hardship in our lives? What does discipline produce in our lives?

2. The Christian life is compared to a race in the above passage. What steps are we to take in order to run our race well? What does it mean to persevere?

3. Read Ephesians 6:10–18. What does it mean to be strong in the Lord and in His mighty power? What actions do we take to accomplish this?

4. Our expectations affect our attitudes. What do you expect from life? How will this affect your relationship with God?

───── CHAPTER 9 ─────

Power from the Holy Spirit

When I went to my Officer Basic Course at Fort Sam Houston, Texas, one of the things I wanted to do while there was learn how to Two-step. Since I attended this course while en route from my internship at Fort Knox, Kentucky, to my first duty station as a physician's assistant at Fort Bragg, North Carolina, most of my personal belongings were in storage at Fort Bragg, including my cowboy boots. So, in order to look the part, I went to the local WalMart and purchased a cheap but nice-looking pair of boots. They looked like real snakeskin. When I wore the boots, I received many compliments on them.

Just like my boots, there are many people today that claim to be Christians, but in truth they are just good imitations. They look genuine and sincere to everyone on the outside, but their spiritual lives are really lifeless and void of the Spirit of God. Their moral standards are high and they are well thought of in the community. They attend church or Bible study regularly and they give money to the church. They were even baptized and confirmed. However, the Holy Spirit does not live in them. The difference between real, true, and powerful Christianity, as compared to counterfeit, mediocre Christianity, is the power of the Holy Spirit. The Holy Spirit is the One Who comes into our hearts and transforms us into children of God.

Jesus dealt with such a man in the third chapter of John. Nicodemus was a Pharisee, and, by definition, a Pharisee was a man of high morals. The Pharisees kept the Ten Commandments and the laws of Moses in order to look holy. A Pharisee was generally well thought of. Yet Nicodemus was not only a Pharisee, but also a member of the ruling council, which means he was like our modern-day Supreme Court justices. As a Pharisee, Nicodemus was required to be present at the daily prayers, attend worship at the temple, make the appropriate sacrifices, and tithe all of his income. If ever there was a man that looked good, it was Nicodemus. But look at the conversation he had with Jesus:

> He came to Jesus at night and said, "Rabbi, we know you are a teacher who has come from God. For no one could perform the miraculous signs you are doing if God were not with him."
>
> In reply Jesus declared, "I tell you the truth, no one can see the kingdom of God unless he is born again."
>
> "How can a man be born when he is old?" Nicodemus asked. "Surely he cannot enter a second time into his mother's womb to be born!"
>
> Jesus answered, "I tell you the truth, no one can enter the kingdom of God unless he is born of water and the Spirit. Flesh gives birth to flesh, but the Spirit gives birth to spirit." (John 3:2–6)

Nicodemus was imitating godliness and he lacked God's Spirit in his life. That is why Christ said he had to be born of the Spirit. We too must be born again of the Spirit. We dealt with that event primarily in chapter one. It is the Holy Spirit living in us that gives us a new heart and enables us to change and become more Christ-like.

Whenever one talks about the person of the Holy Spirit, some controversy and speculation always arise. Is there a difference between walking in the Spirit and being baptized by the Holy Spirit? Does the Holy Spirit still use gifts of tongues and prophecy today? Is there a second filling of the Holy Spirit? How much of our feelings and emotions are controlled by the Holy Spirit?

Everyone's experiences and interpretations of Scripture are often extremely varied, and we tend to think that our experiences and interpretations are the only ones that are valid. The Holy Spirit has been the subject of many debates through the years, with heated arguments over who is right and wrong. These arguments are beyond the scope of this book, but suffice it to say that God, the Holy Spirit, is creative, sensitive, and powerful enough to work in many aspects. What I would like to focus on is what we can agree on as far as the Holy Spirit is concerned. I think we can all agree that the Holy Spirit gives us the power that enables us to live the Christian life in a way that is real and not phony. The Holy Spirit is the One Who makes our hearts new and transforms us.

First, the Holy Spirit living in us is the way God transforms us from sinners to newborn Christians and then to the image of His Son, Jesus Christ. Peter was transformed from a guilt-ridden man hiding in the upper room, from one who cut off the high priest's servant's ear, from one who denied the Lord, to a man who praised God while in prison and stood up to the religious leaders of his day.

The Apostle Paul was transformed from a man who was bitter and legalistic, from one who stood by while Stephen was killed for his faith, from a man who persecuted the church, to a man who established churches all over the world of his time. Joni Eareckson Tada, well-known author and artist, was transformed from a young lady angry at God because of her diving accident to a godly woman who wrote a book entitled *Secret*

Strength and ministers to people all over the world. Chuck Colson, a man known as the hatchetman during President Nixon's administration and who was imprisoned, was transformed so that he is now considered a modern-day prophet by many and runs one of the most successful prison ministries of our time. The Holy Spirit is in the business of transforming hearts and lives.

How does this transformation happen? It is a combination of growth caused by the Holy Spirit and the basics practiced consistently. "Growth" here means being transformed into Christ-likeness, thus being enabled to bear the fruit of the Spirit. "Practicing the basics" means doing what we've talked about in this book on a regular basis. It is a synergistic relationship. Without the basics, the Holy Spirit has no tools with which to produce growth, and without the growth caused by the Holy Spirit, there's no need for the tools.

Let's look at Luke 13:6–9 to understand this better:

> Then he told this parable: "A man had a fig tree, planted in his vineyard, and he went to look for fruit on it, but did not find any. So he said to the man who took care of the vineyard, 'For three years now I have been coming to look for fruit on this fig tree and haven't found any. Cut it down! Why should it use up the soil?'
>
> " 'Sir,' the man replied, 'leave it alone for one more year, and I'll dig around it and fertilize it. If it bears fruit next year, fine! If not, then cut it down.'"

Just as the tree in the parable needed the tools (a shovel and fertilizer) to survive and bear fruit, so you need the tools of the basics (personal relationship with Christ, prayer, precepts, people, praise, perseverance, purity, and the power of the Holy Spirit) to survive and bear fruit in the Christian life. Not only does the tree need the tools to survive, it also needs the loving care and nurturing of the gardener. If the gardener had not interceded for the life of the tree and taken the time to work with the tree, it would not have survived. Just as the tree needed the touch of the master gardener to survive and bear fruit, so you too need the touch of the Master's hand to endure and bear fruit in the Christian life. It is the touch of the Holy Spirit that transforms our hearts.

Another aspect we can all agree on is that the Holy Spirit is real. I want you to think about that statement as I give the following illustration. During my first year of training as a physician's assistant I often had labs for anatomy where I used cadavers. I also used mannequins to practice reviving someone from a heart attack. The first time you walk into a surgical suite to assist with a real procedure, or into an emergency room where someone's having chest pain, the reality and the gravity of the situation grab you, and the knot in your stomach keeps reminding you that this isn't practice anymore.

I often have the same experience in my Christian walk. Everything's going along normally, my prayer and praise times are going okay, the Bible study I'm doing is going well; then out of the blue I have a prayer time or a praise time that is overwhelmingly controlled by the Holy Spirit. It is during these times that the Holy Spirit becomes very real to me.

This happened to me recently while I was studying the healing miracles of Christ. I was studying about the time when Christ healed Peter's mother-in-law, a section of Scripture I had read and studied many times before. (This event is found in Matthew 8:14–17, Mark 1:29–39, and Luke 4:38–44.) After the miracle was performed, at the end of the day, the crowds brought all their sick, lame, and hurting people to Christ for healing. Christ healed many and then quietly slipped away to pray.

Christ was in high demand by the people and He slipped away. His answer to the pressures and high demands on His time and energy was to pray. At the time I was studying this passage, I was overwhelmed with all the demands on my time at work. The Holy Spirit used this Scripture and His perfect timing to both convict me and show me the answer to my busy schedule. The answer was to let the pressures of the day push me to prayer. During that study session the feeling of joy and communion with God overwhelmed me with a sense of peace that I cannot explain. The next day was no less demanding, but I was able to stay at peace because of prayer and communion with the Holy Spirit. The Holy Spirit was working at transforming my heart through everyday life and Scripture. You cannot get any more real than that.

So far we have seen that the Holy Spirit is real and that He transforms us by helping us develop the basics and grow spiritual fruit. Next comes one of the most amazing and hope-filled aspects of the Holy Spirit—He desires weaklings, not superstars! This runs so counter to our culture that we usually do not believe it. We want to have superstars on our side: the smart, the bold, the strong, they're the ones that can help us. To see how ingrained this thought pattern is in our lives, just watch an hour's worth of television and focus on the commercials. You'll be better, look better, and get stronger if you just buy this deodorant or take this vitamin. We see weaknesses as liabilities because the areas in which we fail look unsightly to us, so we see them as unsightly to God. There's the mistake, because the Holy Spirit sees our weaknesses as huge opportunities to reach people and bring glory to God.

Let me show you what I mean. If you look in any muscle-building or diet magazine, you'll see "before and after" pictures of people who've had a big change in how their bodies look because they used a certain diet or worked out a certain way. They always show a picture of someone who lost one hundred pounds and went from a size twenty to a size four dress, or a fifty-inch waist to a thirty-two–inch waist. The more dramatic the change, the more powerful and effective the product looks.

While God isn't in the marketing business, He does want people to come to Him. He joys in taking someone who has a weakness that is visible to the world, using that weakness through which to exhibit His strength, and thereby drawing people to Himself. Lest you think I'm just trying to come up with a way to make us feel good about our weak areas, read what God said through Paul in the book of Corinthians:

> For the message of the cross is foolishness to those who are perishing, but to us who are being saved it is the power of God. For it is written: "I will destroy the wisdom of the wise; the intelligence of the intelligent I will frustrate."
>
> Where is the wise man? Where is the scholar? Where is the philosopher of this age? Has not God made foolish the wisdom of the world? For since in the wisdom of God the world through its wisdom did not know him, God was pleased through the foolishness of what was preached to save those who believe. Jews demand miraculous signs and Greeks look for wisdom, but we preach Christ crucified: a stumbling block to Jews and foolishness to Gentiles, but to those whom God has called, both Jews and Greeks, Christ the power of God and the wisdom of God. For the foolishness of God is wiser than man's wisdom, and the weakness of God is stronger than man's strength.
>
> Brothers, think of what you were when you were called. Not many of you were wise by human standards; not many were influential; not many were of noble birth. But God chose the foolish things of the world to shame the wise; God chose the weak things of the world to shame the strong. He chose the lowly things of this world and the despised things—and the things that are not—to nullify the things that are, so that no one may boast before him. It is because of him that you are in Christ Jesus, who has become for us wisdom from God—that is, our righteousness, holiness and redemption. Therefore as it is written: "Let him who boasts boast in the Lord."
>
> When I came to you, brothers, I did not come with eloquence or superior wisdom as I proclaimed to you the testimony about God. For I resolved to know nothing while I was with you except Jesus Christ and him crucified. I came to you in weakness and fear, and with much trembling. My

message and my preaching were not with wise and persuasive words, but with a demonstration of the Spirit is power, so that your faith might not rest on men's wisdom, but on God's power. (1 Corinthians 1:18–2:5)

Do you get the picture of hope here? We do not have to be wise or intelligent or scholarly. We do not have to be a philosopher or strong or persuasive. We need only to take our weaknesses to God and be available to the Holy Spirit.

This is walking by faith. When you accepted Christ, you did so by faith, and the daily Christian life, or walking in the Spirit, is by faith as well. Living by faith is difficult. It is like stepping off a cliff when Christ tells you to; you do it, trusting that He'll catch you. One of the best definitions of faith I have heard is in the following acronym: Fantastic Adventures In Trusting Him. Walking by faith and following the Holy Spirit to lead involves some risk. It means letting others see our weaknesses, and that makes us vulnerable. Being vulnerable is an adventure in dependence upon God. Think about Jesus— God, the Son, in whom the very nature of God indwelt fully, and yet He became a baby, a child. Talk about becoming vulnerable! What an example that is for us to follow.

The Holy Spirit comes into our lives—comforts us, convicts us, leads us, makes us real, causes growth, produces fruit, gives us spiritual gifts and blessings, uses our weaknesses to glorify Christ, and by so doing, transforms us from the people we are with all the inherent flaws of human nature and makes us like His Son. That transformation will not be complete until we join Christ on that wonderful day in heaven, but it makes us user-friendly while we're here on earth. What do I mean by user-friendly? I mean that we're available to God's love and to love those around us who are just like us.

Praise God for the power of the Holy Spirit Who transforms us and gives us new hearts!

Questions for Chapter 9

1. Read John 3:2–6. How does a person become a Christian? What does it mean to be "born again"?

2. What are the two primary functions of the Holy Spirit?

3. Read I Corinthians 1:18–2:5. Why is the message of the cross foolishness to those who don't have a relationship with Jesus? How does God use weaknesses in our lives? Why does God use the "weak things of the world"?

4. We all have areas of weakness in our lives. What do we need to do with those weak areas?

Epilogue

I hope you see the thread that runs through this book. Christianity—biblical, real and true Christianity—is not about reading the Bible, saying prayers, and going to church. Neither is it simply obeying the Ten Commandments, witnessing to others, and having an emotional high in an exhibition of praise or a religious experience. True Christianity is *experiencing* and *loving* God in our *daily relationship* with Him. I pray that God will become more real, personal, and intimate as you begin your walk on solid ground.

To order additional copies of

On Solid Ground
The Christian Basics

Please send $7.99*
plus $3.95 shipping and handling to:

Susan L. Alspach
c/o William Alspach II
337 West Waterloo Street
Canal Winchester, OH 43110

*Quantity discounts are available